EAST
LONDON
FOOD

East London Food
Second Edition, second printing

First published by Hoxton Mini Press
London 2016

Copyright © Hoxton Mini Press 2017
All rights reserved.

Photography by Helen Cathcart

Written by Rosie Birkett

Design and layout by Studio Thomas

Copyedited by Laura Nickoll

Proofread by Liz Jones

Thanks to Anna D'Alessio and Elena
Silcock for their assistance with the hours
and hours of interview transcribing.
Big thanks to Ruth Brooks for the
extra help and wonderful soup.

Printed and bound by
Livonia Print, Latvia

ISBN: 978-1-910566-05-3

A CIP catalogue record for this book
is available from the British Library.

To order books and collector's editions please visit:
www.hoxtonminipress.com

EAST LONDON FOOD

Written and compiled by *Rosie Birkett*

Photographed and compiled by *Helen Cathcart*

HOXTON MINI PRESS

Hoxton Mini Press

A note from the publisher

What is it about East London food? Everything seems a bit fresher, bolder, less stuffy, more experimental. But Ann and I should come clean: neither of us are foodies. We hardly know a scallop from a scone. But that's what makes it so scrumptious to live here. The food is obviously good – from the bright colours of the salads on Broadway Market to the stone-baked pizza at Crate Brewery on the canal, from the chic-but-cool dishes of Bistrotheque to the Sri Lankan string hoppers at the Pavilion Café overlooking the lake in Victoria Park... you don't need a degree to appreciate the quality.

Is there actually an East London food scene with clear boundaries? Perhaps nothing so exact. Yet there's a palpable energy here, a can-do attitude born of the dynamism and diversity of an area that has encouraged both established and new chefs to take creative risks while respecting tradition; to find new flavours while honouring local produce and seasonal ingredients.

We struggled with the title of this book at first. Initially it was *Modern East London Food* because we were painfully aware of the culinary heritage which we weren't able to cover in depth. But we were also aware of the anti-gentrification brigade; the distaste for expensive coffee shops and white-cloth-clad restaurants. In the end we simply followed our noses and included what we felt and smelt was the very best food we could find. That is why we have covered classic cafés as well as Michelin-starred eateries; young honey producers as well as a seasoned wild forager.

So here it is: our totally biased, utterly exciting take on the people, the places and the recipes of Hackney and beyond. Written and photographed by the brilliant team of Rosie Birkett and Helen Cathcart. This is *East London Food*. Eat it up.

Martin and Ann,
Hackney, 2016.

Hoxton Mini Press is an independent publisher making books about East London. Please consider buying books directly from us:

hoxtonminipress.com

Contributors

Photography by Helen Cathcart

Helen Cathcart is a lifestyle photographer specialising in food, travel, interiors and portraits. After studying photography and art direction in Manchester, she started her career as a photo director in London working on various publications, culminating with a brief stint at British *Vogue*. In 2010 she moved to Sydney to kickstart a transition to being a full-time photographer and was soon photographing for publications such as *Condé Nast Traveller*, *Monocle* and *Australian Gourmet Traveller*. She is now firmly back on Hackney soil shooting for magazines, brands and cookbooks.

Writing by Rosie Birkett

Rosie Birkett is a food writer, stylist and author based in Hackney. She has written features on restaurants, chefs and food trends for magazines and newspapers including the *Independent on Sunday*, *Condé Nast Traveller*, *Jamie Magazine*, the *Guardian* and *Red* magazine. Her recipes have featured in *The Sunday Times*, *Olive* and *BBC Good Food* magazine and she has appeared on *MasterChef* and *Sunday Brunch* as a food expert. Rosie's debut cookbook *A Lot On Her Plate* was published in 2015 to critical acclaim and she was named a rising star by the *Observer* the same year.

Contents

Contents

Foreword

Nuno Mendes

Nuno Mendes is an acclaimed Portuguese chef living in Hackney. He helped spearhead the culinary rise of East London with his supper club The Loft and subsequent Michelin-starred Bethnal Green restaurant Viajante. As well as being the creative force behind the restaurant at The Chiltern Firehouse hotel, Mendes runs Taberna do Mercado in Spitalfields Market.

"I came to East London with purpose. I've lived in a lot of different places, spending time in New York, San Francisco, LA, New Mexico and Miami. The neighbourhoods that I ended up falling in love with and living in – places like the Lower East Side; Brooklyn; the Mission District; Miami Beach – they all had this amazing energy about them. Everywhere you walked, every time you turned a corner, you could see someone expressing themselves in an artistic manner. They were inspiring places to be.

Big cities have big pockets of energy like this, and for me, East London is ours here in London. I've been coming to London since the 80s and I've always enjoyed visiting, but I never really felt the urge to move here until I came to East London. Eleven years ago I came here to visit my oldest friend Jorge and his brother, and I felt an immediate attraction to the place. I remember thinking 'Man, this place has got the DNA of the Lower East Side or Brooklyn', and I went back to New York and said 'I'm moving to London, and I want to try to do a project in East London.'

Most of the time, when I was living in these cities, I was living in the areas I loved, where I could afford to be, but I was working in a different part of the city and I didn't like that. I liked the food but I didn't like the environment. I remember working for a lot of fine dining restaurants in San Francisco and New York and being so completely amazed by the food we were producing, and so inspired by the kitchen environment, but so disillusioned by the dining room. Everybody was on their phone. They would come for lunch here and then go somewhere else of the same calibre for dinner: it was nothing special, it was routine. I thought that the food and creativity of the kitchen was so out of place, so in my dreams I always wanted a restaurant where I could express myself, in an area where the people coming to eat were people I could relate to.

When I first started looking at doing my own project here in London, the first person that I met with was a very famous restaurateur. He gave me a very nice offer at the time, asking if I wanted to do a modern restaurant at a site he had in Trafalgar Square. I went for a tasting with him, we had quite a lot of meetings, and discussed the project, the concept, etc. He was a very nice guy and we got along very well, but at the back of my mind I knew it wasn't really what I wanted to do.

Then there was this advert on Gumtree. It was a very well-written ad, from a guy who had a pub in Hoxton, and I wrote back to him, and we clicked. He wanted to do a gastropub, but I thought we could do something more interesting than that. I had an offer for a significant amount of money, there was equity on the table, a restaurant with a high-profile restaurateur in central London, and then I had this guy that had no experience in restaurants, with a pub in Hoxton. Hoxton was a dead end at the time, it was rough as hell, and this was a big pay drop. But I was like 'Man, I like it! Let's go with it!'

And I remember thinking at the time, 'If I can pull this off, and I can do what I want to do, from this moment on, I'll always be my own person. I'll never be a hired gun.' My CV at the time was representative of someone that could have been easily hired. I had enough experience in different cuisines, I could have been plugged into a kitchen anywhere. I probably would have got on okay, but I wouldn't have been able to do what I wanted to do. So we started Bacchus in Hoxton Square in 2006, and while it didn't last for very long, it led on to The Loft, and then on to Viajante, which I am hoping to reopen on the waterfront in Wapping.

Returning to East London to open Taberna do Mercado in Spitalfields Market in 2015 was a statement of intent for me. East London is my home, and setting up this restaurant here felt like coming home. It's funny that I should use the starting point of my return to the east of the city, where this all began, to come back home to my roots. If I was going to do a Portuguese restaurant in London it would have to be east: my memories of home being reinterpreted in my new home – it's come full circle."

Introduction

Rosie Birkett

It was food that first brought me to East London, and food is the reason I've chosen to make a home here. Where there's good food there's usually a good story, and as a food writer with an insatiable appetite for both of those things, I can't think of anywhere in this city I'd rather live. To my mind, there is no other part of London that lays on such a diverse, vivacious and generous spread. East London is a feast: it's like an all-you-can-eat buffet for your belly and your soul.

I remember vividly my first taste of the East End, on a cold winter night back in 2005. I was living in Leeds at the time, and had come down to London to visit a school friend whose chef-artist boyfriend was living in Hackney, back when chef-artists could still just about afford the rent. He took us for Vietnamese on Kingsland Road and ordered a banquet of tender rare beef wrapped in betel leaves; golden-crusted, garlic-flecked deep-fried soft-shell crab; lace-delicate *bánh xèo* bursting with prawns and beansprouts; and steaming bowls of *pho*.

He showed us how to break chunks off the crispy rice pancake, wrap it in fronds of lettuce and dip it into the sweet, sour chilli blast of *nước chấm*; how to customise our noodle soups with fragrant, unpronounceable herbs before slurping up their savoury, anise-spiked broth. I'd never experienced such a dance of interweaving flavours on my tongue. I'd never tasted anything like it.

When I went downstairs to the toilet I got lost amid a labyrinth of shelving, cardboard boxes and restaurant stock. Behind a makeshift wall of tupperware I stumbled upon a startled, elderly Vietnamese man in

a nightgown tucked up in his bed, watching a flickering television. It was obvious to me at that moment that this place was so much more than just a restaurant serving delicious food. It was a family, doing the best they possibly could with what they had.

And that's what people in the East End have been doing for centuries. Thanks to its proximity to the Thames and River Lea, this part of town was historically always more industrious, and poorer, than the west: built on manual trades like tanning, rope and lead making, tallow works and brewing. Its situation downwind, outside of the original Roman boundaries of the City of London, meant that the potent, noxious smogs from these grimy trades didn't bother the city's rich. It was a community for the proletariat, and for incoming immigrants who could find work and afford the cheaper housing.

Waves of immigration, from the fleeing French Huguenots and first Jews of the 17th century, to more recent settlement of the Bengali, Vietnamese and Turkish diasporas in the 20th century, have contributed a heady richness of cuisine here, from curries and *bánh mì* to *beigels* and *böreks* – the modern legacy of which is explored later on in this book. But perhaps more than any other part of London, the East End has always had its own very distinctive culinary identity. Food has long been a part of the vernacular here – you just need to have a butcher's at the history of its famous eel, pie and mash shops to know I'm not telling porkies.

Forget burgers and burritos: protein-rich eel – one of the few fish to survive the murky waters of the heavily polluted Thames

– was the original street food here. Fished from the river in huge nets and sold from carts in back alleys to nourish working people, they became such a popular dish that shops were set up around them in Victorian times.

Chosen live and writhing by customers, chopped up and cooked in a spiced stock until it turned to jelly, the eels were served along with hearty suet pies, mashed potato and a steaming, vivid green parsley liquor made from the eel cooking stock. Chilli vinegar and pinches of white pepper seasoned the whole lot to perfection. The fact that F. Cooke on Broadway Market, G. Kelly on Roman Road and L. Manze in Walthamstow still do a roaring trade witnesses the longevity of, and ongoing appetite for, this heritage East End Food.

It's perhaps not unconnected that eel makes a regular appearance on the menu at Lyle's in Shoreditch, the modern British restaurant run by chef James Lowe (p.32), which we've chosen as one of the main chapters in this book. Here Lowe uses supple smoked eel he fillets and cloaks in a delicate, eel-infused jelly made with a stock from the grilled eel's skin and head, with apple for sharpness and honey to sweeten. The eel and its jelly is served with the newest, sweetest raw British peas and their pretty pink flowers: it's a dish at once familiar, and yet elevated beyond recognition into something entirely new and exciting. It draws on Lowe's love of distinctive British ingredients, his flair for balancing flavours, and careful cooking techniques indicative of his experience in some of the world's top kitchens.

Lyle's is just one example of the way that the East End's food has progressed and, arguably, overtaken the west when it comes to eating out. Lowe spent four years at the helm at St John Bread and Wine in Spitalfields (p.176), but it was his teaming up with fellow chef Isaac McHale, now of The Clove Club (p.156), in their cooking collective The Young Turks which laid the ground for Lyle's.

The duo cooked a legendary dinner at The Loft Project – the influential supper club of Portuguese chef Nuno Mendes (who we asked to write this book's foreword) on Kingsland Road, before launching into an ebullient residency above the famous local boozer The Ten Bells pub in Spitalfields.

Here you had two chefs, both of whom had spent time in world-class restaurants including The Ledbury, The Fat Duck, Noma in Copenhagen and Marque in Sydney, cooking accessibly priced gastronomic food with flawless British ingredients. The music was loud, the waiting staff were equal parts charming and mischievous, the nights ended with too much Poire William and – though my memory from that time is hazy – dancing on tables. Both chefs now have Michelin stars and globally-acclaimed restaurants in the East End.

Like Mendes, who first cooked his own dishes at his short-lived (but well-remembered) Bacchus restaurant in a disused pub in Hoxton, the cheap rent and open-mindedness of the east gave these young chefs a platform, enabling and nurturing their nascent careers into what they've now become: shifters of the British food scene.

As well as basic geography, it's this DIY spirit - this enterprising, kinetic, can-do culinary creativity - that binds the heterogeneous mix of people, places and foods in this book together. The brilliant characters who depict this energy range from the talented and entrepreneurial Vietnamese cook Uyen Luu at her supper club in Hackney, to mother and son team Urvesh Parvais and Lalita Patel, who create authentic renditions of their family recipes at Gujurati Rasoi in Dalston.

We discover an organic, volunteer-run urban farm overlooked by council estates in Stamford Hill, and meet Ben Mackinnon, the man who set up one of London's best artisan bakeries in a disused railway arch in London Fields. We meet self-proclaimed 'Cockney It-ies' (pronounced 'eye ties') Anna and Nevio Pellicci, whose family café E. Pellicci in Bethnal Green has been the backbone of their local community for over a hundred years; and step inside Palm² in Clapton, a Turkish, family-run corner shop which has moved with the times to compete with its local Tesco.

There are chefs galore, from the Michelin-starred likes of Lowe, McHale and Mendes, to Alex Szrok, who cooks single-handedly in a functioning butcher's shop on Broadway Market. Down the road we find Claire Ptak, a Californian pastry chef who's adopted Hackney and its wild produce, working locally foraged ingredients into her flavoursome bakes, and we discover young food start-ups like Sandows London in Hackney Wick and Square Root sodas in Hackney Central, who are riding the wave of this culinary exhilaration.

On page 100 you'll find Jonathan Cook, or 'John the Poacher', as he prefers to be known. John splits his time between caring for elderly and infirm people in his community, and foraging, mushrooming and poaching his way around the council estates of Hackney and the surrounding marshland, selling the produce to local cafés, restaurants, breweries and food start-ups. John has lived in the area for decades, and he remembers a very different East End to the one we know today, but his knowledge of the wildlife and vegetation in the area, taught to him by the old boys who used to hunt with dogs in the marshes, offers us a connection with the place that transcends time.

Since interviewing him on a three-hour foraging walk, I see wild food growing all over East London, something that as a cook excites me beyond words, as I greedily await the seasons and the bounties they will bring. I would never have expected to find ceps, wild garlic or quince growing wild in East London, and there's a lesson there about never underestimating what this remarkable area and its generous people have to offer.

I didn't realise it at the time, but I've been researching this book for the last eight years. That's the time that I've been working as a jobbing food writer in London, and as I've written features and reviews for magazines, websites and newspapers, I've felt the gravitational shift of the food scene eastwards, and moved with it. Researching the book has been a delicious voyage of culinary discovery, but it's also been an enriching personal exploration, and many of the characters I've met while writing it – characters like John, for example – have educated and inspired me in ways I never imagined.

I hope you too feel inspired as you read these stories and that you enjoy this snapshot of modern East London food – for a snapshot is what it is. We couldn't possibly have included everything good and food related that is happening, because there is so, so much going on, but rather we've given an overview of some of its highlights, all beautifully illustrated by Helen Cathcart's stunning photography. Bon appétit.

Lyle's

"Once you've seen something be as good as it can be, there is no other way."

James Lowe, Founder and Head Chef, pictured.

To say that chef James Lowe is a stickler for detail in his approach at his modern British restaurant Lyle's in Shoreditch is an understatement. His focus, and tireless thirst for knowledge and pursuit of the best British ingredients, coupled with the natural charms of business partner and front-of-house manager John Ogier, have meant that in the short time since it opened in May 2014, Lyle's has topped best restaurant lists across the world, notched up a Michelin star and – more significantly for the Lyle's team – garnered a following of die-hard denizens.

The restaurant's location in Shoreditch is important. It's just around the corner from friend, former Young Turks collaborator and co-chef Isaac McHale's Clove Club (p.156) and highlights the eastward shift of culinary excitement. Like Isaac, James is at the forefront of an energetic new generation of British chefs who are changing the game for British gastronomy.

This generation are creating restaurants for their peers, rather than for expense accounts, and with its jolly, attentive staff and kinetic open kitchen, this place goes light on pomp and ceremony, but heavy on the detail. At Lyle's, which is named after James's grandmother, the tone is informal yet professional, the vibe is fun and inclusive and the food is some of the best you'll find in the UK, but accessibly priced, with the four-course set dinner menu a steal at under £50.

"It's produce led, it's British, there is a modern approach, it's pared back and all the food is very common sense," says the chef. For James, this 'common sense' approach is the most important thing, and he uses it as a catch-all term to explain why he cooks seasonally; sources fruit, meat and dairy direct from farms (often going fruit picking himself); buys in whole animals to butcher; and wastes very little. Meat from acclaimed Cornish butcher Philip Warren is bought in, already aged, to keep in the significantly sized fridges to improve its flavour and texture further. "Properly aged meat tastes better, so why wouldn't you?"

"The food is very simple, but getting to put food that's that simple on the plate is not simple," says James. "To get to that point you have to say 'no', and 'that's not good enough' to an awful lot of things. That's down to the skill of the chef. To be able to hang a piece of pork for three months you have to have a butcher that's got the right facilities, the pork has to come from the right farm, and then you have to cook it on a charcoal grill, and it has to be served pink. It's a terribly simple plate, but really truly, brilliant simple food is not simple. Take a slice of Spanish *jamón* – behind it is two years of work, and generations and generations of knowledge."

While all the dishes are focused on, and based around, seasonal British produce from treasured suppliers, the food at Lyle's also takes in the wanderlust of James's twenties, much of which he spent travelling and cooking, so there's a Basque-style charcoal grill for searing; a Japanese approach to clean, layered stocks and sauces; and a New Nordic nod in his use of foraged produce and herbs. Beautiful sourdough bread is made in the restaurant every day and served with another house speciality – deeply flavourful cultured butter. Every element – from the sleek mid-century vintage Ercol furniture to the carefully chosen wine and rotating coffee selection – is a showcase for excellence and craft.

Getting a Michelin star the year after opening, despite Lyle's' clear rejection of the formality usually favoured by the guidebook, might seem like a dizzyingly fast ascent, but for Lowe, Lyle's has been a very long time in the making, its success the culmination of years of working towards opening his own restaurant.

"The desire to have a restaurant came before the desire to cook," says the chef, who

"I didn't want to open my restaurant somewhere I didn't live or like."

began his restaurant career in East London as a waiter at the legendary, now-defunct Wapping Project. He was working there after university while interviewing with British Airways to become a pilot, but his career plans were scuppered when airlines stopped recruiting post 9/11.

"After a couple of months of cooking at the Wapping Project I wasn't thinking about flying any more. All I could think of was, 'Where am I going to work next? How am I going to get to my goal of opening a restaurant? What's the next path?'" James worked at restaurants including The Fat Duck, where he cooked for 18 months; Noma in Copenhagen, where he did a brief stage; and St John Bread and Wine, where he spent four and a half years as head chef. It was here that he met John Ogier, and developed a particular penchant for game, something Lyle's celebrates extensively during the season on its menus and with special guest chef dinners.

After leaving St John Bread and Wine he went on to travel and cook his way around the world before joining forces with Isaac McHale, himself fresh from the kitchens at The Ledbury, to form the Young Turks collective. They cooked their creative British food together in a series of irreverent pop-ups and suppers before taking over the upstairs at East End pub The Ten Bells, winning acclaim both locally and globally. It was during this time in 2010 that Lowe began to search desperately for his own site.

"I was more uncompromising than you should be when looking for a restaurant site," admits James. "It took years, but I didn't want to open my restaurant somewhere I didn't live or like. It had to have decent natural light and the kitchen had to be open. When I first walked into the Tea Building with John my initial thought was, 'we absolutely cannot lose this site.'" And we're all very pleased that they didn't. "I'm one of those people that when I've seen something really good, I can't go back: once you've seen something be as good as it can be, there is no other way."

Lyle's:
Tea Building
56 Shoreditch High Street
London E1 6JJ

Website:
lyleslondon.com

Follow:
@LylesLondon

Asparagus, chicken vinaigrette, buckwheat and Burford Brown egg. See recipe section at back for details.

Gujarati Rasoi

"The food we make today is still reflective of the food that was made in rural India a great many moons ago."

Urvesh Parvais, Co-founder, pictured (right) with Co-founder Lalita Parvais.

Disappointed by the generic fare offered by most Indian restaurants in London, Urvesh Parvais longed to share the food of his heritage and his childhood – the fresh, textural and under-represented Gujarati food he grew up enjoying – with his local community in Hackney.

The lineage of Urvesh's family food goes back to the region of Surat in Gujarat, India, a pious state where vegetarianism is part of the religion, and the resulting cuisine is some of the most tantalising vegetarian food in the world. While Urvesh's great grandparents moved from India to East Africa in the 1940s, bringing up his mother Lalita there, the recipes of their homeland were fiercely guarded by the family, resolutely followed and lovingly rendered in order to keep their culinary tradition alive.

When his mother moved to the UK in the 1960s, she continued to cook those recipes to the letter at home, passing on that passion to her son. "The food has maintained its integrity because of that movement across many continents and the nostalgia inherent in that food. It had to taste that way or it wouldn't taste of home and of India."

"It's time-capsule food because of that fact. It's pre-Industrial Revolution, pre-processes. Everything is made by hand, locally and with seasonally sourced ingredients. It's come full circle. These ideas are ancient. Processes and methods are very important and make the food what it is, and it's crucial not to cut any corners in that regard."

After holding a tasting of his mother's food that delighted his friends, Urvesh was spurred on to learn his mother's recipes, and eventually gave up his job as a designer in order to cook, setting up a weekly market stall on Broadway Market in 2004, selling a short menu of their Guajarati snacks and dishes. "I talked my mother into working with me – she's my link in terms of recipes and techniques – but she didn't under-stand the skill and value she had initially. We put together a menu and stall which was very humble, put our food and ourselves out there, and what was amazing was that the crowd in Hackney almost ten years ago understood it."

"We had one pot and one idea, but over the months our confidence grew and we learned to work together. So many people who came to the stall were well travelled, and many people had been to India more than I had. It was nice to be able to speak about our food in the vernacular of how we spoke at home, and to see how people understood it."

Working at the market and food festivals, mother and son saved up enough money to build a kitchen in Hackney to service their stall and another stall they set up at Borough Market, followed by the restaurant in Dalston which opened in 2012 with Urvesh in the kitchen and his mother giving creative direction and development. "The food we make today is still reflective of the food that was made in rural India a great many moons ago. It hasn't changed; the only difference is that we can get better-quality produce here," he says.

The cosy, simple restaurant recreates the intimate feel of eating in an Indian home, with an open kitchen at the back where you can watch Urvesh tempering spices in sizzling oil and plating his fragrant dishes. The seasonally changing menu is short and focused, with just three choices of starter, main and dessert, but some mainstay dishes that people come back for again and again.

One such dish is the *papri chaat*, a cravable confluence of different textures and tastes, with crunchy *chorafari* ribbons made with nutty gram flour fried until crisp. This is mixed with black chickpeas that have been cooked with ajwain seeds, topped with a fresh, zingy raita with crushed mustard seeds, cucumber and lemon.

"There's an energy in East London which is DIY – a sense that 'we can do it, we can put something out there in the world which is unique ...'"

Chopped onion, coriander and pomegranate seeds with date and tamarind sauce add sourness, sweetness and freshness. "It's a flavour explosion, and one of our signature dishes. There would be a riot if we took it off the menu."

A glorious version of the ubiquitous dish of *palak paneer* is made with delicate homemade paneer, peanuts, chilli, ginger and spinach, and is best washed down with a cumin-spiked salted lassi or the house cocktail of gin and fresh lime juice sweetened with jaggery syrup.

Urvesh is infectiously proud of the food he creates at the restaurant and market stalls, and of his location in this stretch of Hackney. "Part of the reason we're in Dalston is that we knew people in East London would be open-minded and receptive. There's an energy in East London which is DIY – a sense that 'we can do it, we can put something out there in the world which is unique – let's use our creativity as we haven't got the cash'. There's lots of people out there with that approach: if they're not building it they're appreciating it, and they're not bothered if your floor isn't perfectly polished concrete. We were still screwing things into the wall the night we opened, and we only had 12 covers, but we made it work and now we're a busy restaurant with 40 seats and we're looking for more sites."

Gujarati Rasoi:
10C Bradbury Street
London N16 8JN

Website:
gujaratirasoi.com

Follow:
@GujaratiRasoi

Taberna do Mercado

"We were thinking about holding back on the pork fat, but I made the decision not to. I want this food to be real. It's bold, and it's got punch. I'm not going to apologise for that."

Nuno Mendes, Chef and Founder, pictured (right) with Head Chef Antonio Galapito.

Pig trotter and cuttlefish coentrada. See recipe section at back for details.

After blazing onto the East London scene with his brilliant but short-lived restaurant Bacchus in Hoxton Square, back in 2006, Nuno Mendes got everyone talking about his influential Loft Project supper club and subsequent Michelin-starred restaurant Viajante in Bethnal Green. When it closed in 2014, Mendes launched the restaurant at the glamorous Chiltern Firehouse hotel in Marylebone, and the softly-spoken, perpetually understated Portuguese chef went from being the name on the lips of the culinary cognoscenti, to being the name on everyone's lips.

It was somehow surprising then, that he should return to East London with the opening of Taberna do Mercado in 2015: a small, humble, all-day restaurant in Spitalfields Market serving Portuguese custard tarts, house-tinned fish and rustic pork loin sandwiches. But, as the chef tells us, coming back to East London was "a statement of intent".

"Opening a restaurant in East London felt like coming back home, because East London *is* my home," explains the chef. "I wanted Taberna to have that connection to place, and I wanted to do a project about accessibility. It's in this market in a thriving part of East London, and it's a place you can come in, at any time of day and have an offering – whether it's a coffee and a custard tart; a sandwich to take away, or a sit-down dinner. It's taking me back to street level."

His head chef here is Antonio Galapito, a fellow Portuguese native who's been cooking with Mendes for years. "Tose has been with me since the Bacchus days. He first came over to stage with me there when he was 17, and slept on the floor, and he's one of my oldest allies. I wanted this to be his restaurant too – to give him a kitchen, visibility and space to grow. His family have suckling pigs in Portugal which we will use on the menu soon."

Taberna is a carefully conceived homage to Mendes' roots, translating and elevating the gutsy Portuguese fare of his childhood with the aplomb you'd expect from a chef of his form. His 'house-tinned fish' references the popularity of tinned fish in Portugal, but uses pristine British seafood paired cleverly with flavourings that enhance them in tins like scallops with brown butter and walnuts, or monkfish cheeks with garlic and shallots.

Dishes draw on what Mendes calls the 'punch' of his native cuisine – you'll find small, memorable plates like the cuttlefish and pig's trotter: sweet, clean pieces of cuttlefish swimming in a porky, gelatinous broth heady with coriander and white pepper. This is rib-sticking food that could set you up for a day in the fields: there's an abundance of the country's staples of egg yolks, pork fat, bread, olive oil and coriander, and they're all rendered in an intelligent way.

"Returning to East London was a statement of intent for me."

Taberna do Mercado — E1

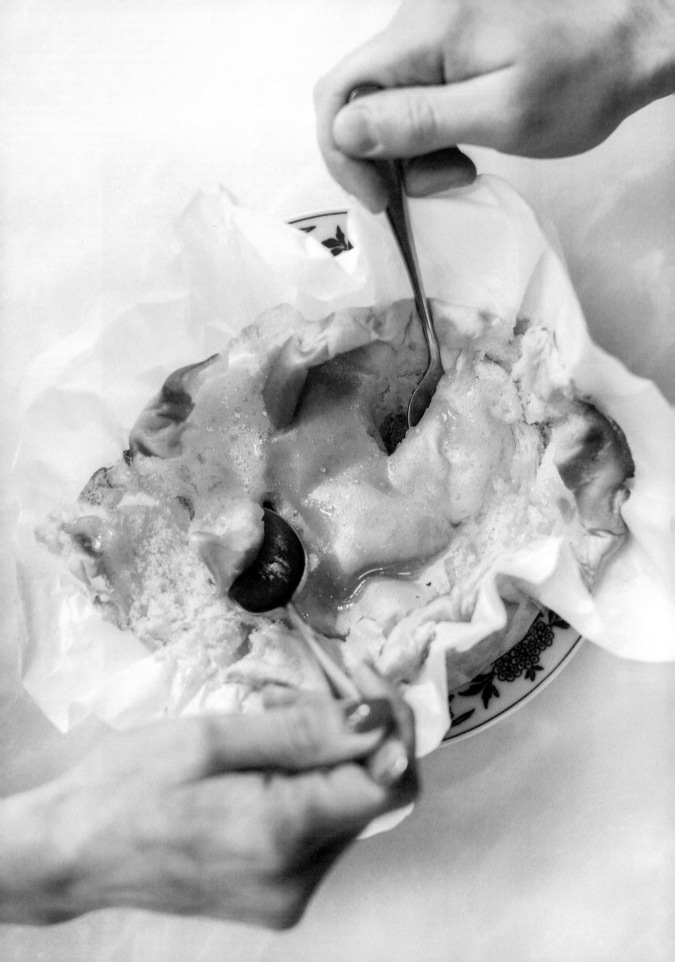

"We were thinking about holding back on the pork fat, but I made the decision not to," says the chef. "I want this food to be real. It's bold, and it's got punch. I'm not going to apologise for that. It's good-quality products treated well, but it has a very specific DNA."

And there's certainly no need to apologise for a glorious dessert of steamed egg yolks and pork fat that comes in a shimmering slab atop a slick of aromatic port caramel. Another dessert of olive oil and runny egg sponge comes encased in greaseproof paper and is served to share. It's the sort of dish that will have you fencing your dining companion with a dessert spoon across the table.

"It's considered," Mendes says of the food. "The moment I set out to do a Portuguese restaurant outside of Portugal I had to look at tradition, but also observe it from afar. I'm not in Portugal, it's my memories that are here." And those memories are translated on to the menu with more than a whiff of Proustian recall. The custard tarts, whose yolky, silken centres ooze out on to the plate once cut into have gained a cult status all of their own within London, but for Mendes, they're rooted in a very specific moment, of another time.

"We serve our custard tarts with a spoon because they are deliberately undercooked and runny," he says. "That comes from when I was a kid and used to go to the café with my grandmother. She would always have a really strong Portuguese espresso, and I would steal her coffee spoon and use it to eat my tart, spooning out the middle before eating the crust. We serve them like that to maximise the enjoyment of eating them."

Mendes clearly gets a kick from sharing these personal little details with his diners, and there's a real sense of pride and purpose in Taberna's food, with the chef relishing the chance to showcase his country's cuisine and products. "For such a small country we have incredible food," he says. "That prawn paste that we put on the beef prego sandwich – that is something that started in Portugal, travelled to India, morphed into something which is used in Goa all the time and came back to Portugal. It's fascinating."

While he wouldn't dream of using anything but British runner beans for his tempura-fried fritter clusters with clam and coriander juice, Mendes goes to great lengths to import some of the best produce he can from Portugal to share with Londoners, bringing in beautiful olive oils, artisan wines, Violet prawns from the Algarve, goose barnacles and even its beloved Super Bock beer. "It's the beer no one drinks outside of Portugal but everyone loves. You have no idea how difficult it was to arrange to have it on draft! We serve it ice cold, just like you'd have on the beach."

Taberna do Mercado:
Old Spitalfields Market
107B Commercial Street
London E1 6BG

Website:
tabernamercado.co.uk

Follow:
@tabernamercado

E. Pellicci

"It's not just a caff, it's a meeting place. It's the only place left in London where people actually communicate."

Jukebox Jimmy, Regular customer.

Anna Pellicci, Maria Pellicci, cousin Tony Zaccaria and Nevio Pellici.

So often, walking into a café in East London can be a hushed and self-conscious affair, as solo visitors pore over their laptops with their pour-over coffees and serious expressions. Not at E. Pellicci. Here, the morning rush (which lasts until the lunchtime rush) is alive with chatter, laughter and the clamour of fast, jolly service: there's not a computer screen in sight.

Everyone who comes through the door gets a welcome, usually from Nevio Pellicci, his sister Anna or their cousin Tony, who slip casually in and out of Italian as they chat to customers and shout out orders. Portraits of their Italian grandparents Elide and Priamo, who opened this café back in 1900, flank the service hatch at the back of the restaurant where their mother Maria is still cooking at the grand age of 75.

People share tables and conversations while they sip the well-brewed leaf tea and tuck into fry-ups, or – as some regulars prefer – Maria's famous pasta dishes. Maria makes simple, generous café food from scratch every day, and is known for her homemade béchamels, ragùs and pestos. Her glorious lasagne comes by the huge, molten bowlful and is easily enough for two people to share – a steal for under £8.

"She still chops all her chips by hand, makes all the pies from scratch and makes all the pasta sauces," says Anna. "Mum came over from Italy when she was 21, like so many people, looking for work, got a job here in the caff and subsequently married my dad. The poor love's been in the kitchen for the last 56 years. She's brilliant. It's good, home-cooked food at a reasonable price."

The café is ornately decked out in antique wooden panelling that was carved by local carpenter and café regular Achille Capocci in 1946, though at the time the family could only afford to pay for and instal it a panel at a time. The art deco design of the panelling was out of step with the trend for American diner-style décor that most cafés were adopting, but it has been preserved beautifully and resulted in the building achieving Grade II listed status.

Nevio Senior, who ran the café up until he died, was born in one of the rooms upstairs, and the family grew up here, descending on the café for mealtimes and mucking in with jobs from the age of 11. "Before school and after school we were always here," says Anna. "Years ago when my dad and uncles were alive, before we went home we'd have a lovely big meal out the back with my grandma, when that part of what is now the kitchen used to be the living area. Most nights even when my children were young we'd come here after school, and about 6pm all sit here and have something together."

While Anna has tried her hand at other jobs, working in an office for four years, the pull of the family business proved too strong to resist. "I love being in here," she says. "Ultimately, we're doing it for ourselves and our children, like our parents did for us. We work hard but we don't work half as hard as my parents and their parents before them. When I think about the hours my mum used to work – they were here at four in the morning, six out of seven days a week. We want to pay our respects to them and keep it going. We've been asked to expand and become a chain but I think it would lose its warmth if we did that."

When you sit in E. Pellicci, you need to be prepared to be sociable, because the unwritten rule is that everyone talks to everyone, and the mix of clientele makes for compelling conversation. "It's such a hub in the community," says Anna. "The demographics in the area have changed so much over the last 20 years but we get everyone coming in here. You get your trendies from Shoreditch sat next to Jukebox Jimmy, who's a proper cockney bloke, involuntarily at first because the caff's busy, but so many lovely friendships have grown out of that."

"Ultimately, we're doing it for ourselves and our children, like our parents did for us."

Jukebox Jimmy can be found sitting at the same table at the back of the café at approximately the same time every day, unless it's raining. "I have to sit at this table, because this, out here," he says spreading his arms out before the café. "This is cabaret."

"I'm a music man, that's why they call me Jukebox Jimmy, and this is my second home. I've been coming here for 50 years and it's the best caff in London. It's not just a caff, it's a meeting place. It's the only place left in London where people actually communicate. When you're sitting next to each other, you can't fail to hear what people are talking about next to you and join in their conversation, that's how it is. Nevio and Anna are always welcoming, and their dad was the same. It hasn't changed a lot. I would bring my kids and grandkids and that's how it's always been, families bring generations of kids in here. That's how it goes on."

For Anna, a warm welcome is crucial to the café's success as a business, and to its proud East End heritage. "The East End has always been known for its warmth and welcome and I do think that's in danger of being lost. The area has always been a place for anyone and everyone, and this café reflects that. We're from an immigrant family, and that's what I've always loved about it here. Every little bit of whatever adds a flavour and makes it richer."

"Some of the new places have an attitude that you're doing them a favour for going in there, but that's not in the spirit of things. That's how the East End always got through – the community – and if it goes, I don't know ... Half the people who come in here, I know if I needed something, they would help me. If it goes too far the other way and loses that, it would really upset me."

E. Pellicci:
332 Bethnal Green Road
London E2 0AG

Bistrotheque

"Everything I have done has been influenced
by my time going to The Haçienda in one
way or another."

Pablo Flack, Co-founder.

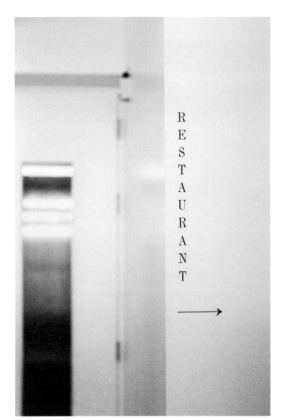

With its glorious flower arrangements, gleaming white tiles, carafes of pale pink bellini and tinkling grand piano, Bethnal Green's Bistrotheque is a stylish place to eat, whether for piles of pancakes for brunch or a roast chicken dinner. But, as unlikely as it might sound, this influential and scene-shifting East London restaurant had its genesis in the most unglamorous of places: a service station car park just outside Wakefield. It was here, in 1991, at a post-rave after-party at Woolley Edge services, that Pablo Flack and David Waddington met for the first time. Just over a decade later they would spark a dining revolution with the launch of their legendary avant-garde diner Bistrotheque.

"In the northern club scene, because they would close quite early, you'd go to a rave and then go to a car park for a party. I'd always have a certain number of drugs for the club and a certain number for the service station car park," says Pablo Flack, who had been at The Haçienda club in Manchester on the night that he and David met.

It wasn't until a few years later, however, that the two would reconnect when they both worked at the famous Bricklayers Arms bar, itself a sort of clubhouse for the young creatives at the epicentre of the cultural eruption in mid-90s Shoreditch. Both men ran the bar throughout its busiest period, before breaking out on their own and launching their first joint venture, Bistrotheque in Bethnal Green – at the time a desert for dining.

"It was kind of a reaction against what was going on in Shoreditch," says Pablo. "I'd bought a flat further out, in Well Street, and people were moving out – it was the first wave of displacement. At the Bricklayers, there were hundreds and hundreds of people out in the street in the end; it just sort of exploded. It had become really mainstream and the thing about us is that we're not particularly mainstream operators. We like things that are busy, but we like our own little world at the same time."

The nascent restaurateurs found their site – a former factory that produced "knock-off Burberry ponchos" – and fell in love with its incongruous location and industrial character, itself redolent of the clubs they both frequented. "It was a sort of gothic, dark, moody street, so much so that taxi drivers wouldn't stop and let people out. When we opened, the fact that there was food on a plate in this location was quite rare. People were thankful that it was a warm room with electric lighting and food was coming out of the kitchen! There was very much a feeling that it was the deepest darkest Hackney at this point," says David.

The duo cite the influences of rave culture as a factor in why Bistrotheque drew the crowds from the get-go. "People weren't scared about going to a party in the middle of nowhere, so having a restaurant in the middle of nowhere made total sense to us, whereas probably to the generation of restaurants above us they had to be on a certain street with a ground floor presence,"

"I'm not into fussy, dainty, smeary food. I just want to cook things that people want to eat."

Pablo Flack and David Waddington, Founders.

says Pablo. "Rave just changed all those rules: rave culture is the reason we're here."

When the restaurant opened in 2004, resplendent with chic white linen and flowers, table service and classical dishes with a whiff of luxury, it was a pointed rejection of what the pair call "sloppy East End standards". "We felt like that was really missing in the East End when we started," says David. "I think we came up with a good edit of it that suited a younger generation but it was all underpinned by some sense of properness."

Another draw was the space beneath the restaurant, which grew into one of London's most influential alternative cabaret venues. Pablo had invited drag performer Johnny Woo from New York's Lower East Side to start a lip-synching night, and it became a cult event and a key part of the cabaret revival, drawing in drag queens and cabaret performers from across the world.

The irreverent cross-over of the alternative performances, the industrial grandeur of the dining room and the toothsome French–British bistro food created a uniquely hedonistic vibe for which Bistrotheque became known, attracting locals in their hoards, as well as the global fashion glitterati and Hollywood stars like Scarlett Johansson. Over the years David and Pablo have harnessed their knack for decadent dining to branch out and run immersive pop-ups and food events across London, more recently teaming up with the Ace Hotel in Shoreditch to create its restaurant Hoi Polloi, which launched in 2013.

The cabaret room at Bistrotheque came to a natural end in 2012 when the pair decided to remodel the venue and concentrate solely on the restaurant side of the business. "We thought we'd better stop while we were ahead. We've grown up now, and so have our audience. You can constantly chase the new kids, but that seems a bit unseemly to me! It's more important to know our audience and ask 'What do these people want now?'"

Though they claim death threats would be likely if they no longer offered some of the more classic dishes like the steak tartare, the restaurant's young head chef Jackson Berg has a pretty free hand when it comes to planning the menu. He's inspired by his grounding at British restaurant St John, and Hoi Polloi, and uses British seasonal ingredients to come up with modern plates like salt hake, heirloom tomatoes, chicken aïoli and cauliflower. "I'm not into fussy, dainty, smeary food," says the chef. "I just want to cook things that people want to eat. It's tasty, honest food."

Having blazed the trail for East London's restaurant scene, Bistrotheque is no longer an isolated bastion of quality food in the area, but it still stands alone, thanks to Jackson's faultless cooking and David and Pablo's unique history. "We have every admiration for other restaurateurs around us, and we adore the fact it's so foodie – it makes everyone up their game," says Pablo, "but I think that there is a slight difference between us and the newer generation. They are taking everything much more seriously but for us, restaurants are about having fun, and having a party, and we try not to forget that."

Bistrotheque:
23–27 Wadeson Street
London E2 9DR

Website:
bistrotheque.com

Follow:
@BISTROTHEQUE

Salt hake, heirloom tomatoes, chicken aïoli and cauliflower. See recipe section at back for details.

Barnes & Webb

"A beekeeper that says they haven't made a mistake is either a miracle worker or a liar."

Chris Barnes, Co-founder, pictured (left) with Co-founder Paul Webb.

On the bright, artfully designed homepage of East London-based nomadic beekeepers Paul Webb's and Chris Barnes's website is the confident message 'Beekeeping, the easy way', along with their promise to instal and maintain beehives, and share the harvest of delicious local honey 'without any of the hassle'. Allowing green-inclined urbanites the satisfaction of housing beehives in their gardens or on their roofs, along with a steady supply of the honey created with nectar from their locale is a brilliant idea. But these two former designers would be the first to admit that mastering the mysterious, ingenious ways of the honey bee has been anything but 'easy'. "It's impossible not to make mistakes," says Chris. "A beekeeper that says that they haven't is either a miracle worker or a liar. We've got stung loads; we've lost swarms; and I've killed a queen. I felt dreadful!"

"I think we've been quite lucky overall though," admits Paul. "The most important thing to us is the welfare of our bees. If that's compromised in any way then we don't do it, which can be not so great for business, but I wouldn't want to do it any other way."

Both residents of East London, Paul and Chris met years ago as budding designers working at the same agency, and their fascination with beekeeping began when they em-barked on a short course together. This led to more courses, and eventually to Chris moving to Auckland in New Zealand to work a summer season on a bee farm. "I persuaded him to start doing a blog on his experiences while he was there," says Paul. "It was just fascinating to read, and I was sort of living vicariously through his experiences. So when he came back and said 'we can do that here', I didn't need convincing. We had both worked in design for 15 years, in various different roles, and it's just a lot of bullshit really! We were sick of it and just wanted to do something that has some kind of meaning to it."

They set up the company in 2013, running it from their shared house in Homerton, with Paul still running his own design agency on the side (which he's since shut down) and Chris doing a bit of freelance design to subsidise the slow and unpredictable growth of their venture. While they initially focused on renting out their hives and beekeeping services, now it's their award-winning small-batch, unpasteurised Postcode Honey that has become the focus.

"As soon as we started getting our honey out there after the first season we realised that the huge demand for local London honey far outweighed the actual supply," says Chris. "When you buy honey in the supermarket it's

"We realised that the huge demand for local London honey far outweighed the supply."

pasteurised, and it's a blend of honeys. With ours it comes out of the hive and we put it through a sieve – there is nothing else done to it. The bees do all the work."

Mimicking the working cycle of the honey bees, the pair work long days throughout the summer, maintaining the hives in order to harvest the honey at the end of the season, in late August or early September. Their honey sells out almost as soon as it has hit the shelves, thanks to its rich, interesting flavour: the result of London's varied, year-round flora. "It's got a complexity to it because the bees have access to such a wide variety of different types of nectar," explains Paul. "While heather or lavender honey is delicious, you know exactly what it's going to taste like, whereas we have no idea from one year to the next what that honey is going to taste like. It's totally dependent on what the hive decides as an organism it will forage."

It's also prized for its perceived alleviation of hayfever symptoms. "Hayfever sufferers go mad for it because the traces of local pollens are supposed to help them. We had pre-orders for it this year and it's been really difficult keeping up with demand."

The pair now manage over 20 hives in East London alone, including some in the scenic gardens of Shoreditch's Geffrye Museum, with each hive's honey taking the name of its post-code. And while they still have to keep their toe in with freelancing over the winter, becoming urban beekeepers has drastically improved their quality of life. "I didn't really notice the seasons before," says Chris. "But now I'm more in tune with them because of what I do with the bees all through spring and summer. I notice the flowers and I notice the seasons, and when Paul and I are sitting in a little room, covered in honey and working until midnight, or up at 5am moving bees, it still doesn't feel like work."

For Paul it's about finding something he really believes in. "All my life I've strived for what I do for a living to have some integrity, and I've found that really difficult. But with something like beekeeping you can't change it; it is what it is. Like with any kind of farming you have to work symbiotically with nature for it to be properly successful, so you have to give yourself over to those things, and that is beneficial to you and to the environment that you're working in. There is this lovely symbiosis between people and bees: it's a mutually beneficial thing."

Barnes & Webb—N16

Website:
barnesandwebb.com

Follow:
@BarnesandWebb

London Borough of Jam

"I like to use unusual additions such as bay leaf, cardamom, liquorice and wild fennel pollen, which enhance the fruit flavours and create natural, respectful combinations."

Lillie O'Brien, Founder.

Lillie O'Brien, Founder.

To Lillie O'Brien, heaven is an afternoon spent making loganberry jam. "They're my absolute favourites, and one of the reasons I love summer here so much," she says, with a wide smile. "I only use fruits when they're in season, which is why when you come into the shop in January or February everything is orangey-coloured – it's all marmalade and lemony preserves."

Australian-born Lillie's zeal for the fruity gifts of the British seasons is witnessed as soon as you set foot in her delightful shop, the London Borough of Jam. Situated just off the increasingly food-focused Chatsworth Road in Clapton, and open at weekends only, LBJ is a cavern of thoughtfully sourced, quality food and drink goodies curated by the former St John Bread and Wine pastry chef.

At the core of her business are her seasonal, small-batch jams and preserves which sing with creative flavour combinations such as 'Blackberry and bay leaves' and 'Greengage plum and fennel pollen'. These are sold at the shop and also supplied to shops, delis and restaurants such as Selfridges, Violet (p.188) and Leila's Shop. Lillie describes her jams as "fruit-driven, rather than sugar-driven", and she cooks them for much less time than conventional, large-scale jam producers, in order to let their character really shine. "I like to use unusual additions such as bay leaf, cardamom, liquorice and wild fennel pollen, which enhance the fruit flavours and create natural, respectful combinations," she says.

Outside the front of the shop, Lillie sells good pour-over coffee, local craft beers and well-priced carafes of decent table wine for customers who want to linger. Her talent for textiles and design, which she studied before going into food, makes for a compact but beautifully laid-out space inside, with hand-woven African bolga baskets hanging from the ceiling along with dried fennel, bay and oregano leaves that she's collect-ed on her travels throughout Europe. Weighty food journals, carefully selected cookbooks and striking ceramics from Puglia sit alongside organic handmade tea towels from Australia and bean-to-bar chocolate from the Pump Street Bakery in Suffolk.

"Everything is in here for a reason. I'd never have anything in here that looked good but didn't taste good – I'm really conscious of that. If you have quality you gain trust from people, so they come to your shop again and again and believe in what you're selling."

The diverse, globally-sourced nature of her wares reflects Lillie's own journey to this corner of Clapton. Having grown up in Melbourne, she abandoned textile studies in favour of working in food, starting an apprenticeship with a family friend who was a chef, working in restaurant kitchens locally before taking a job in Japan. In 2008 the UK beckoned, and Lillie snared a job at one of East London's most exciting restaurants, St John Bread and Wine, where she embarked on her career in pastry.

Working with the then-head chef James Lowe (now of Lyle's – p.32) and Japanese pastry chef Kenta Ohki, she became part of a tight-knit crew. "I stayed for four years. We had loads of fun. Now when I look back on it and I look at all the people that worked together, who are doing all these amazing things, I think 'Oh my God, that was such a special time.' I used to sort of bounce off James with my dessert ideas. He'd order things in – I'd never seen a loganberry before, or a wild plum, or bilberries – and would be like, 'I've ordered these, they're amazing: do something with them!'"

The fiercely British, seasonally driven philosophy at Bread and Wine found Lillie busily preserving during more fruitful months, and discovering a penchant for jamming. "We had a big dry store in the cellar and it would have a section

"If you have quality you gain trust from people. They come to your shop again and again and believe in what you're selling."

where we would just put loads of things in big giant Kilner jars: mainly jams and stewed fruits, and it made sense because they were in their prime. That way, when winter came around we'd make raspberry ripple ice cream, or steamed sponge with the jam, and it meant we had something. I like that – you don't really have anything and you have to make do."

Today, she splits her week between the demands of running her own business – the research, stock organisation and ordering – and making jam (the wholesale side of things is based in a small jam factory in Suffolk), opening her shop for the weekend. Having lived down the road from the shop for years with her husband Marcus and cat Chester, LBJ is a home-from-home, and Lillie's love for her borough is evident, not least because it led her to the name for her business.

"I was looking for a name, and my friend Daniel Willis (of The Clove Club, p.156) suggested an inspiration trip to the Hackney Archive. We went around there and just sort of looked at books and tried to get ideas, and I didn't find anything. It wasn't until the end that it came to me. I had a book and I saw the library stamp that said 'London Borough of Hackney' and I just thought, 'hang on a minute ...'"

London Borough of Jam:
51D Chatsworth Road
London E5 0LH

Website:
londonboroughofjam.com

Follow:
@LdnBoroughOfJam

Sager & Wilde

Sager & Wilde Wine Bar:
193 Hackney Road
London E2 8JL

Sager & Wilde Restaurant:
Arch 250 Paradise Row
London E2 9LE

Website:
sagerandwilde.com

Follow:
@sagerandwilde

Visionary husband and wife team Charlotte and Michael Sager-Wilde launched their buzzing, defiantly unstuffy wine bar on Hackney Road in 2013, repackaging wine appreciation for millennials. Daring to open and sell fine and rare wines by the glass, the couple pulse with obsessive enthusiasm for interesting, terroir-driven wines. While the bar offers simple snacks like grilled cheese sandwiches, terrines and pickles, their sister Sager & Wilde Restaurant on Paradise Row in Bethnal Green boasts hot young chef Sebastian Myers (previously of Viajante and The Chiltern Firehouse) in the kitchen, and his original, well-priced set menus are as exciting as the expertly curated wine list.

Rochelle Canteen

"I LOVE lamb tongues; they are gentle, forgiving
– lovely offal. A tongue has had a good amount
of exercise from eating grass. People sometimes
think offal is dirty; well, anything in the head
is definitely clean."

Margot Henderson, Co-founder, pictured (left) with Head Chef Anna Tobias.

Having lunch at Rochelle Canteen is captivating and enchanting all at once, and it's something you'll find yourself yearning to do repeatedly once you know about this special hidden place. Set in the white-washed converted bike shed of a former Victorian school in Arnold Circus on the handsome Boundary Estate – London's first social housing development – it's a delicious, incongruous pocket of serenity amid the frenetic hustle of Shoreditch.

Accessed by ringing the buzzer on the door in the estate's characteristic red-brick wall, once inside you'll walk through the schoolyard, past foxgloves and foliage to a simple, modern space with a focused, unfussy menu of brilliantly cooked seasonal food. If it's summer, sit outside and admire the pots flush with homegrown lovage and lettuce, and the fig tree whose leaves will infuse custard for ice cream. In winter, sit in the warmth of the open kitchen, rich with the smells of slow cooking, and note the jars of preserves from more fecund months.

The restaurant's name refers to the fact that it is unlicensed, only open for lunch, and was initially set up as a makeshift canteen for the local workforce of artists and designers by business partners Margot Henderson and Melanie Arnold. "My friend James Moores owns the building and said we could base our catering company here. We had a fridge, an oven on wheels and a bench, and we just moved from one room to another, doing catering jobs while our kids were running about," says Margot of the early years.

"Then we opened the canteen. We had one table that everyone shared, and then we thought we'd better get more tables and chairs and a credit card machine, and it grew out of necessity. No one knew about it, but they came quite quickly. Giles Deacon was based here and the fashion world brought a lot of press – they liked the link of the two things together. We're in this beautiful spot, with the lovely green grass: you feel a bit like you're on holiday."

Beautiful though the space is, the main draw here is Margot's food: the fruit of a lifelong career in restaurant kitchens. She came to London in her twenties from New Zealand, where she'd been cutting her teeth cheffing, having come from a family of food lovers: her mother had written books on local eating houses. "She had a passion for eating, but she was quite into health food when I was young. We had a lot of brown bread, bran muffins and molasses so I slightly rebelled and started cooking white biscuits, meringues and things for my brothers, and I enjoyed it. I think I was always a bit greedy. I've always loved restaurants and thought they were great; from a very young age I thought 'this is the best place to be, in a restaurant, being served by people'."

While her preference as a young girl was to cook up French-inspired garlic snails, Margot's food is now synonymous with British cuisine. She met her husband – the revered British chef

"We're in this beautiful spot, with the lovely green grass: you feel a bit like you're on holiday."

Fergus Henderson – while working at The Eagle gastropub in Clerkenwell, and before long the couple were married and, famously, cooking together upstairs at Soho's The French House.

"They were giddy days. We were madly in love! His food was so brilliant and different. I couldn't believe it – I thought it was so crazy. He'd say, 'we're not going to bone out the quail, we're just going to cook it whole', and at that time no one did that. I was still picking sprigs of parsley and putting them on as a garnish, and he said 'oh no, we're not doing a garnish', and I thought that was so fantastic. He taught me about traditional British cooking, which I'd never done – cooking a whole British ham, slowly, 'blip, blip, blip', and you know, just more about gentle cooking, cooking the whole animal, and it all really made sense."

When Fergus went off to open St John with Trevor Gulliver and John Spiteri, Margot continued as executive chef at The French House, where she still worked with Arnold until the pub decided it could run its own dining room. In 2006, they came to Shoreditch. "It's changed massively," she says of the area. "We don't get bricks thrown through the window any more, but there aren't that many artists about either. That's part of cities: they change and you can't hold them back. I do think it's sad it's not council housing any more here, but it's a great area and there's lots going on."

Working with head chef Anna Tobias (previously of the River Café and Blueprint Café), Margot creates short, seasonal menus that sing with confidence and simplicity. "I just follow our instincts. It's food that should have an effortless feel. It's nice if it has an influence of Britain around it, though we do slip around a bit."

The canteen's manager Alcides Gauto has his own distinctive service style that's earned him his own cult following. "He's been here so long and people love him; even when he's grumpy, people love him," laughs Margot.

For Anna: "It's uncomplicated and good and it's just a relaxed place, both as an employee and for people to have lunch – you relax when you come here. There's also a lot of comfort food. We do things like sausage and potato salad. That's not the most exciting or modern dish, but it's good. I think a lot of people sometimes want to have a lunch where it's simple and unfussy and you're not required to consider the plate too much."

Rochelle Canteen:
Rochelle School
London E2 7ES

Website:
arnoldandhenderson.com

Follow:
@Rochellecanteen

Lamb's tongue, green beans and green sauce. See recipe section at back for details.

Beigel Bake

Beigel Bake:
159 Brick Lane
London E1 6SB

Though the street is famed for its curry houses, the Ashkenazi Jews brought beigels to Brick Lane in the 19th century, and thousands are still freshly made here each day. At Beigel Bake, which serves the rolls with holes 24 hours a day, they are boiled and then baked in the traditional manner, and stuffed with salt beef, gherkins and hot mustard, or lox and cream cheese.

John the Poacher

"I live on Pot Noodles. Wild food is only good for selling – I wouldn't waste it on myself."

Jonathan Cook, Wild food expert, pictured.

"Everything's legal until you get caught."

With its stark pylons, graffiti-sprayed concrete, barbed wire and backdrop of housing estates, the allure of East London's sprawling marshes could be lost on some. But, as unconventional a pastoral landscape as it is, there's a brutal beauty to this flat, overgrown expanse that teems with diverse wildlife and plant species.

Depending on what time of year you visit Walthamstow and Hackney Marshes, you can find kingfishers, herons, horses, butterflies, water voles, adders and even belted Galloway cattle chewing the cud. You might also catch sight of a rarer specimen: a tall, wily man in a check shirt and oilcloth hat carrying an extendable ladder under one arm and a bucket under the other. To Jonathan Cook – known locally as 'John the Poacher' – the marshes are a vast allotment, rich with wild food that he hunts, forages, harvests and sells on to locals, restaurants, pop-ups, box schemes and food and drink producers.

"I didn't grow up in the country. I moved to London and learned my trade," says the self-taught forager. Born in St Helens on the outskirts of Liverpool to parents who ran Salvation Army hostels, John moved around the country as a child until his family settled in Upper Clapton on the edge of the marshes, in the house that he still shares with his mother.

"We've been in the same property for the last 31 years." This lengthy residency becomes apparent when you stroll around the area with John, who seems to know everyone. He's renowned in the community – not just for the snared rabbits and wild mushrooms he sells at local boozer,

the Anchor and Hope, but through his work as a carer and odd-job man for the elderly.

His true vocation, however, lies in finding wild food in unlikely places. He canvasses not just the marshes, but housing estates, parks and canal paths for his haul. "People don't look on their doorsteps," he marvels. "You have different nationalities turn up and they throw different things out the window so you get different plants and stuff growing. I've got almond trees and violet patches in council estates, but I won't tell you where they are."

"Springfield Park has the most diversity in terms of the species you can get in there. You get all sorts. And so many mushrooms. I've had ceps, chicken of the woods, beefsteak fungus. I pick in excess of 120kg per season just in Springfield."

John is playfully protective about what he calls "my marshes", but does run foraging walks to teach small groups about the joys of finding wild food. "I like teaching people," he says. "I'm trying to make the walks more regular, to stockpile the money and buy a boat. I get all sorts of people coming, from locals to bankers and lawyers. They love to see where the stuff comes from that they've been paying through the nose for at the farmer's market."

Spending time with John opens your eyes. You see maple, oak and walnut where you once just saw trees; sloes, blackthorn and gorse where you once glimpsed hedgerow. You'll find startlingly peppery wild rocket growing at the canal's edge and fronds of astringent fennel by bridges. If you know where to look, a bountiful

"Autumn's my favourite time of year, because you get all the fruit and the mushrooms. But I like winter best because you don't get so many arseholes about."

larder awaits: from sweet violets and primroses, fragrant elderflower and wild garlic to yellow bullace plums, pears, blackberries and quince. "I know these marshes better than the back of my hand and I'm always out and about finding things. I even pick on Christmas Day."

While he taught himself about foraging from reading books, the knowledge John has of his local area and what to poach from it was passed on to him by the "old boys" who took him under their wing as a lad. "I was never really one for socialising with people. I always used to come out here as a kid on my own, fishing, and there were a few old guys that I used to hang around with out here, who used to hunt rabbits with the dogs. They taught me. Two of them are still around; the others have passed away. One of them still does a bit with a catapult. It's not strictly legal, but everything's legal until you get caught. It's a very effective method if you're good at it – I've seen them get pheasants out of trees."

John occupies his own space somewhere between old and new Hackney, caring for older people in the community who have lived here all their lives and remember a very different East End to the one we know today, but also servicing the savvy young start-ups who crave the produce he seeks out. He supplies Square Root London (p.108) with the elderflower and cherry blossom for their seasonal sodas, and proudly has his own dandelion and burdock porter with local craft brewery Pressure Drop.

Though he professes a love of Pot Noodles, John's diet is supplemented by what he can get his hands on in the wild, be that by donning Marigolds to pick nettles for potato and nettle soup, or shooting mallards and wood pigeons for supper.

"Wood pigeons are good throughout the year, and tasty. If it's a choice between going to the supermarket and spending a few quid on bad chicken or going and shooting a wood pigeon, I know what I'd choose. I'd cook it up with nettles and wild garlic."

Follow:
@jonthepoacher

Square Root London

"We began by making some fermented ginger beer, based on a really old recipe, and tweaked it week-on-week until we were happy with it."

Robyn Simms, Co-founder, pictured (left) with Co-founder Ed Taylor.

Walking into the railway arch where Square Root make their remarkable, seasonal small-batch sodas, you're immediately hit by two things: the intense smell of whatever fruit or veg they happen to be pulverising to extract the juice, and the whirring sound of the huge stainless-steel tree shredder they use to do it. Beside the shining tanks are pallet upon pallet of produce – everything from Yorkshire rhubarb to cucumber or bergamot – waiting to be transformed into delicious drinks to be stocked by shops, restaurants, pubs and bars locally and across London.

It's amazing to think that this operation, which now produces up to 2,700 litres of soda during a busy week, started life as a weekly market stall. Bored with her job in a bar, Robyn Simms started playing around with making her own drinks to sell with partner Ed Taylor at their local market. "We began by making some fermented ginger beer, based on a really old recipe, and tweaked it week-on-week, refining it and squeezing out the juice to get a fuller flavour; finding ways of making it taste better until we were happy with it," she says.

The couple experimented with more recipes using seasonal produce, purchasing a 100-year-old tricycle and fitting it with kegs and taps to cycle their creations to the market each week. They joined street-food collective Kerb and traded across London, where the drinks proved so popular people would come with bottles to fill up to see them through the week. Robyn quit her job and spent a whole summer trading, figuring out ways to make the business sustainable throughout the winter, and turning to citrus fruits when seasonal ingredients were scarce.

Ed left his job as a brewer at Howling Hops brewery in Hackney, and the pair used a start-up loan and all their savings to set up their soda production facility in Hackney Downs, calling on metal-worker contacts they'd made through their brewing experience to design their bespoke kit. "By the time we'd set up and bought all the equipment we only had enough

"By the time we'd set up and bought all the equipment we only had enough cash for one pallet of stock ... We made the first batch, sold it in order to make more and grew it from there."

cash for one pallet of stock," says Ed. "We made the first batch, sold it in order to make more and grew it from there."

As well as sourcing produce direct from farmers (often using misshapen fruit that would otherwise be discarded) to create seasonal sodas like raspberry lemonade, rhubarb, cucumber and apple, they call on local forager John the Poacher (p.100) for ingredients such as elderflower and cherry blossom to make special limited-edition drinks. They've also perfected a year-round, core range of drinks based on inventive, natural versions of what people want at a pub: a ginger beer, lemonade, root beer, cola and Cascara Club soda. The soda is a collaboration with Climpson and Sons Roastery which imports Bolivian cascara – the coffee berry husks – a by-product of coffee production that gives coffee farmers another revenue stream.

Ed used to do a lot of work with community food projects, and he's keen to incorporate a social responsibility element into the business, working with social enterprises which take people who have never visited a farm to pick fruit for sodas. "It's so nice to be able to work with social enterprises to actually help them along. We're getting revenue so it works for both of us. It's really fun – the blackcurrants they pick come from a Ribena farm and would otherwise be wasted. They make a beautiful soda."

Website:
squarerootlondon.co.uk

Follow:
@squarerootldn

Uyen Luu

"You can love feeding people, but doing a supper club on the scale I do has to work as a business."

Uyen Luu, Chef, pictured.

Uyen Luu must struggle to fill in the tiny boxes on forms that ask for your job title. 'Culinary creative' is probably the best catch-all term to describe her effervescent career, which entails her working as a food stylist, writer and photographer, as well as an accidental chef, cooking for a staggeringly successful supper club from her flat in Hackney every weekend. She's also somehow managed to fit in having her daughter Olive and writing a critically acclaimed cookbook, *My Vietnamese Kitchen*, but then, creating opportunities through food runs in her family.

Luu was born in Saigon just after the war in 1977, and her earliest memories of her motherland revolve around the food there. "After the war people had their businesses taken away by the communists, and one of the ways to make money and survive was to open your house up and sell food," she says. "My grandmother was a great cook and entrepreneur, and she turned her front room into a restaurant, selling *bún bò huế*, a spicy, lemongrass-scented beef noodle soup. I remember clearly the wonderful way it tasted."

Fleeing the devastation in Vietnam in search of a better life, Luu's mother Le brought her and her brother to Hackney in the early 80s, where she settled among the Vietnamese diaspora and brought them up single-handedly. Growing up in the East End among the artists that made their home in her community – drawn by the cheap rents and cheap but tasty Vietnamese restaurants – inspired Luu to go to art college, and she studied filmmaking at Central Saint Martins before opening a fashion boutique in Covent Garden.

Her supper club, which was one of the first in London, started in 2009 after she realised that she was cooking and hosting so much in her flat, she might as well start charging for it. "I decided to do it because I always held dinner parties anyway," she says. "This was just another step up from that."

It was also driven by a frustration at a lack of home-cooked quality she perceived on the Vietnamese restaurant scene. "I felt like no one was cooking up to any standard that I was enjoying. My mum is such a good cook, so she came to help and teach me. What better way to share the cooking with her and make everything really tasty? I'm still learning from her."

Incredibly, Le had never really cooked until she moved to London. "In Vietnamese families among the female children, one is assigned the cooking, and the other siblings are assigned an education," explains Luu. "My mum had a sister and it was her who was the cook, so Mum was more of an eater; she didn't really cook. She's got a good palate and she learned from the Vietnamese community here, from friends and from her own mistakes."

At the centre of Vietnamese cookery are theories of heating and cooling through food, and also balancing principles of yin and yang, which the Vietnamese believe is at the centre of nutritional and emotional wellbeing. Together, Luu and Le cook a set menu, a procession of hot and cold courses that navigate diners through the taste and textural interplay of Vietnamese cooking, traversing and perfectly balancing the smooth and the crunchy, the sour, sweet, salt, umami, bitterness, spice and zingy freshness of the cuisine.

Dishes veer between traditional recipes like the silken pork and rice pancakes *bánh cuốn*, or her famous beef *pho* – arguably the best in London – and more modern ideas like her inspired 'raw fish and chips' (soy and orange marinated tuna with twice-cooked chips and wasabi mayo).

Over time, Luu's supper club garnered a reputation as the best place to eat Vietnamese food in London, and with fans including Jamie Oliver and Raymond Blanc, who both rave about

"My grandmother was a great cook and entrepreneur, and she turned her front room into a restaurant, selling *bún bò huế*, a spicy, lemongrass-scented beef noodle soup."

Luu's cooking, reservations have been coming in thick and fast for years. "I never anticipated the interest the supper club would get," she says. "It grew out of good word of mouth and luck, and it became a business. You can love feeding people, but doing a supper club on the scale I do has to work as a business. All this has led to me being a professional photographer, stylist and writer. It was a mad dream at the start; in fact, I didn't even dare to dream it! I just wanted to cook for people."

While she's looking to relocate her studio and supper club to make more room for daughter Olive and photographer partner James O'Jenkins, Luu is fiercely proud of her neighbourhood, and intends to keep her operation in Hackney. "It's changed tremendously since we came over from Vietnam but I'm happy and privileged to see that change and to have grown up here and been a part of that. I love it in East London – there's so many places to eat and loads happening. It's really interesting to be living here, and be inspired by others and having all the other cultures here. I feel lucky to be in the mix of the food scene here."

Website:
uyenluu.com

Follow:
@loveLELUU

Chicken noodle soup. See recipe section at back for details.

Palm ²

"If we'd just carried on doing the same things as Tesco we never would have survived … We've had to move with the times."

Suleyman Solak, Chef.

They don't make local shops like Palm^2 on every street corner. In fact, they don't make shops like Palm^2 anywhere except for this particular street corner overlooking Clapton Pond. Local shops that sell pints of milk and tins of beans don't usually double up as delis with counters of still-warm roasted vegetable salads, oozing lasagnes and golden, garlic-and-rosemary-flecked chicken thighs. This bustling food emporium has everything food lovers could possibly crave, from freshly baked pastries and locally roasted coffee, to rainbows of good-looking ingredients, fresh seasonal vegetables, artisan sourdough and Neal's Yard Dairy cheeses. There are fridges full of craft beer and there are organic wines aplenty, but it also sells stamps, batteries and boxes of tissues.

The latter nods to the fact that Palm^2 started life as a simple corner shop, a quarter of the size it is now. Set up in 1994 by the Turkish Solak family, it was flanked by a café and a bookies. "It just used to be a normal corner shop selling average things that all the local shops do," says Suleyman, whose father and uncle set it up and who now cooks in the open kitchen at the back of the shop with three other chefs. "They started to get a lot of customers and it was going well so they decided to buy the café and bookies next to it and knock it through. When Tesco opened just next door they decided to change the business to more of a deli with Spanish and Italian food and things like cheeses, olives and nice produce. If we'd just carried on doing the same things as Tesco we never would have survived."

Suleyman came over from Turkey to join his family in 2004, and after training as a chef at Westminster College and then working at renowned French restaurant Mosimann's in Knightsbridge, he joined the shop. "The area has changed so much for the better in the last seven years," he says. "It used to be called murder mile around here but there are a lot of families here now so there was the need for a place like this in the neighbourhood. It's been 21 years and a very long process and it's evolved. We've had to move with the times."

It takes an incredible amount of self restraint to walk into Palm^2 and not be tempted by the food that Suleyman and his co-chefs have cooked up. Even if you're not particularly hungry when you go in, you will be once you've feasted your eyes on the colourful platters of fresh food, or once the savoury waft of just-baked *böreks* has wafted up your nose. "If we run out of the *böreks* people are asking for them," says Suleyman, who goes to New Covent Garden market three times a week to source the shop's ingredients and stock.

As well as the food cooked by the chefs that's for sale in the shop, the event space on the first floor of the building transforms into a breakfast café at the weekends and hosts a roster of different cuisines cooked by roving chefs, food start-ups and street food vendors in the evenings. Across the Lower Clapton Road, Organic and Natural is the little sister of Palm^2, which joined the ranks in 2009 and lives up to its name by specialising in organic, vegan, gluten-free and special dietary requirement foods

Suleyman Solak, Chef.

127

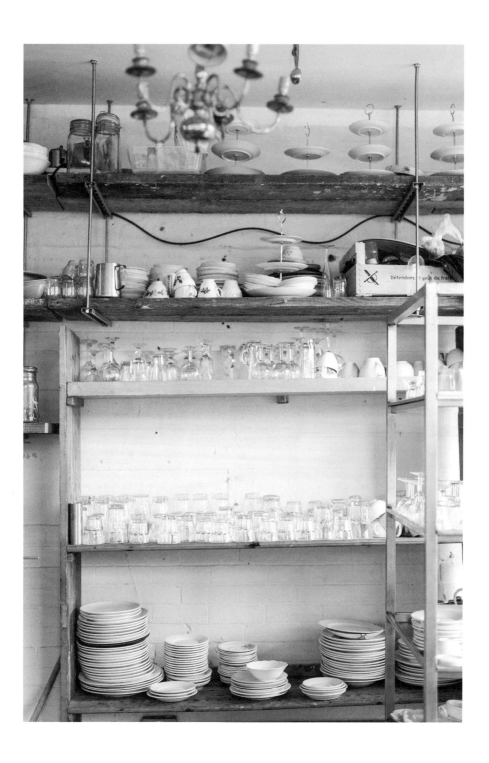

"It's been 21 years and a very long process. The area has changed so much for the better in the last seven years."

and supplements. There's a food counter there too which is serviced by the kitchen team at Palm², and like its flagship, the shop sells wares from local suppliers and small producers like E5 Bakehouse (p.146) and Growing Communities (p.178) along with organic meats from Rhug Estate in Denbighshire and juices, salads and vegetables from Chegworth Valley Farm in Kent.

"We have a lot going on with the events space and the organic shop," says Suleyman. "We've thought about expanding outside of Clapton but when I think about how much work we've put into it and how it relies on everyone – my uncle, my father, my wife and everyone who works for us – you have to be on top of it all the time. We will keep it small and good quality rather than growing any more. There's a real sense of community and family atmosphere here and that's not something you find in other parts of London. I know kids who are six or seven years old who I knew when they were in their mothers' tummies. Having those relationships with the people around you is really special."

Palm²:
152–156 Lower Clapton Road
London E5 0QJ

Website:
palm2.co.uk

Follow:
@palm2eventspace

Imam bayildi (stuffed aubergine). See recipe section at back for details.

Verden

"We've been planning this on some level all our lives, and we're obsessed with the details."

Ed Wyand, Co-founder, pictured (left) with Co-founder Tom Bell.

Childhood friends Tom Bell and Ed Wyand grew up two streets away from each other in North London, in a group of food-obsessed friends who fantasised about one day having their own restaurant. Fast forward a couple of decades and the pair can now be found in a handsome former pub in deepest Clapton, running their joint venture. A sleek, gleaming ode to modernist Japanese and Scandinavian design, Verden is a playground for the palate that begs you to settle in and surrender yourself to its charms: be that a glass of carefully selected wine and a plate of cuttlefish croquettas at the bar, or a full-on feasting menu.

"We talked about food and restaurants much more than you'd expect normal teenagers to do," says Tom, who left a successful career as a PR director to open his first restaurant together with Ed (previously second maître d' at Scott's) in June 2014. "We've been planning this on some level all our lives, and we're obsessed with the details. We wanted to do something that's accessible from a price point of view, but also serve food and wine that's interesting, unusual and has a great story behind it. Our philosophy was very much 'think global, act local' – it's about journey and discovery and we set out to go and find the best ingredients we could possibly find. Everything has to have some point of distinction."

As such, Verden offers one of the most exceptionally curated wining and dining experiences in East London, in a buzzy Clapton neighbourhood setting and with a price tag lower than you might think. A plate of charcuterie will set you back a fiver, while wines by the glass start at £4.50. You could decide to ease in with a glass of sparkling pollen cider from Hertfordshire for £4, or a flute of cloudy, natural Veneto prosecco for £7. If you're feeling more flush, the sparkling gamay d'Auvergne makes a glass of champagne seem like a comparatively prosaic choice, and is still fantastic value at £8.

"Because we're not spending £200k a year on rent, we can afford to do something really interesting, and really different, without charging Mayfair prices," says Tom, who along with Ed is a self-taught wine enthusiast with an infectious interest in small producers. Together with the help of young, visionary wine importers like Tutto and Gergovie Wines, they've created a list that features 30-odd wines by the glass and 70–80 bottles. The list features natural, organic and biodynamic growers and small wineries across the Old and New World who have been chosen for their unique and expressive bottles.

"Wine is starting to catch up with food in terms of people being interested in provenance," says Tom. "It's about finding quality and a point of difference. Gone are the days when restaurants had to work with one or two suppliers from big commercial wineries who supply you the whole list. These are wines that we love to drink and we're thrilled to be sharing them with our customers."

The same rigorous approach to sourcing is applied to design elements like the elegant, hand-carved leather-backed bar stools, handmade by local, Clapton-based furniture maker Pippa Murray; and of course the food, which relies on suppliers like acclaimed native-breed butcher Philip Warren in Cornwall, and Ed's own family farm in Lincolnshire.

From November through to January, the farm provides game birds for the menu. "Seasonality is key, and we try as much as we can to use things that make sense to use," says Ed. "My grandfather started a shoot in the early 60s with a bunch of Lincolnshire farmers and we shoot four or five times a year. We had a family shoot last weekend and came back with 60 birds, mostly pheasant and mallard, but sometimes we also have wood pigeon and woodcock. It's an incredible thing to be able to bring to Verden."

"Wine is starting to catch up with food in terms of people being interested in provenance."

During game season the chefs have fun with the wild produce, creating specials like pheasant kievs and wood pigeon with pickled mushrooms, along with game scotch eggs, pheasants on horseback, terrines and game pies. Throughout the year, dishes are based around a few pristine seasonal ingredients, taking flavour influences from around the globe. The menu might include squid and 'nduja on squid ink-slathered toasted sourdough; bavette with grilled radicchio and blue cheese butter; or burrata with peaches and heritage tomatoes.

"This restaurant is modelled on how Ed and I like to enjoy ourselves, so it feels very personal: it's an extension of our personalities," says Tom. *Verden* translates as 'world' in Danish, and speaks of the way the founders scoured the globe for inspiration before they opened. "For us restaurants are not just about food and wine, they're about the experience. We've travelled a lot and we've cherry-picked the best bits from cities like Copenhagen, New York and Paris, where relaxed, informal neighbourhood dining is done with incredible quality."

Verden:
181 Clarence Road
London E5 8EE

Website:
verdene5.com

Follow:
@VerdenE5

Verden—E5

Almond milk producer
Haggerston

The Pressery

"We wanted to do one thing, do it our way, and do it really, really well."

Chi-San Wan, Co-founder.

Finding something original to bring to London's burgeoning food and drink scene is an almost impossible task in these days of creative street-food start-ups, where ideas spread like wildfire on social media. But when food-obsessed friends Chi-San Wan and Natali Stajcic discovered a shared love of fresh, handmade almond milk – free from industrially-produced additives – they knew they were on to something.

Fast forward a couple of years and the savvy duo now have their own wildly successful cold-press almond milk business, The Pressery, that supplies the likes of Selfridges and The Chiltern Firehouse as well as local cafés and delis.

"We have a mutual group of friends but we were always the ones that sat there banging on about food together," says Natali, who was struggling with the inflexible hours demanded by her music management job after having a baby. "Chi was tired of fashion, and there was this one night – I think it was her birthday – where we both decided to quit our jobs and do something together in food."

"I remember us thumping on the table yelling 'let's do this!'" says Chi, who had been making her own fresh almond milk at home for a while because she was disillusioned by the quality of almond milk available in the shops. "I used to live above a health food shop and buy almond milk in cartons and just end up thinking there's nothing really 'healthy' about it: there are very few almonds, it's really sweet, it doesn't taste like almonds, and it's gloopy with thickening agents."

Driven by this desire for a nourishing, delicious alternative to non-dairy milks, both as a base ingredient and as a drink, the pair began researching what was on the market, and discovered that no one else was making almond milk in London. "We learned that many of the leading brands making almond milk were only using 1 to 2 per cent almonds per carton, and we couldn't believe that no one else was trying to make it here, so we just knew we had to hurry up and get on with it," says Natali. Enabled by a business loan from the East London Centre for Small Businesses, they bought some cold-press machines, sourced some organic almonds from Spain and set up shop in the basement of Curio Cabal café in Haggerston, making raw, activated almond milk. "We wanted to do one thing, do it our way, and do it really, really well, but when we started making it we quickly realised why no one else was doing it like that!" says Chi, referring to the gruelling production process involved in hand-making the milk.

Starting at 6am on their production days, they would cold-press the soaked almonds for hours using purified water before transferring the pulp and juice into muslin bags and then squeezing out the white milk by hand. They would then put the milk into chillers – old slush puppy machines – leaving the original just as it was, and adding natural flavours to the rest: cacao sweetened with vanilla and dates; turmeric and cayenne balanced with raw honey; and berries (raspberries and blueberries).

Because of the unpasteurised nature of the product, it only had a four-day shelf life, meaning they had to deliver it to stockists on the day it was made. "It was a massive barrier," says Natali. "We were told we would never get it into shops. But within two weeks of selling the bottles Daylesford (the organic farm shop) got in touch via social media and wanted to get a sample." The response to their milks, whose vivid (but wholly natural) colours shine from their chic, minimally branded plastic bottles, has been so overwhelming that Natali and Chi pushed themselves to the limit in terms of what they could physically produce themselves, supplying a host of loyal clients who put up with the stop–start supply and brief shelf life.

142

Natali Stajcic and Chi-San Wan, Founders.

"It is a delicious drink. It should be on shop shelves, it should be in fridges. We're not trying to replicate the texture of milk because it's not milk; it's a different thing."

"We were producing it with domestic machines because that's what we could afford, and we reached 6,000 bottles a month making it ourselves, but then the machines began smoking and starting to pop off in our faces and we knew it was time to move this to the professionals."

Tapping into their huge social media following – built up mostly through their stylish, playful Instagram account – the pair crowd-funded investment to help scale up their business, outsourcing production to a better-equipped facility, and increasing the milks' shelf life to 21 days through carefully trialled pasteurisation that uses pressure, rather than heat, to preserve it. This has allowed them to make their flavoured milks available outside of London and the UK, and deliver a consistent volume to loyal and new suppliers, without compromising on the quality of the milk.

They've also developed a pure, long-life organic almond milk aimed at coffee shops, supermarkets and suppliers looking for a quality dairy alternative with a longer shelf life. "We're growing slowly, because we can't grow any faster – we don't know how to. It's our baby. And every so often we do open a bottle and go 'Okay, this is really great'!"

Website:
thepressery.co.uk

Follow:
@thepressery

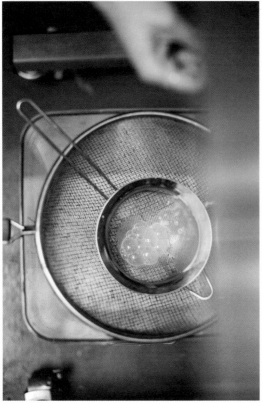

E5 Bakehouse

" The more you learn about sourdough the more you realise that we shouldn't eat any other kind of bread."

Ben Mackinnon, Founder.

Ben Mackinnon, Founder.

" I am incredibly proud to be a baker. Bread has been the backbone of our communities for years."

"My intention was to have one hand in the bread bowl and one on the laptop, and do renewable energy as a freelance consultant. But I very quickly fell in love with making bread for people, and the freelancing went out the window," says Ben Mackinnon, founder of East London's best-loved bakery, E5 Bakehouse. Set in a spruced-up disused railway arch in London Fields and known for its slow-fermentation breads, particularly its 'Hackney Wild' sourdough, E5 Bakehouse is an organic bakery, café and shop serving simple meals based around its delicious baked goods.

Mackinnon left his career in renewable energy to begin baking after learning about the wonders of slowly fermented, naturally leavened breads at a week-long course at the School of Artisan Food and Wine. "I left utterly converted," he says. "The more you learn about sourdough the more you realise that of course we shouldn't eat any other kind of bread. Fermentation causes a pre-digestion of the food compounds so we can extract a lot more nutrition from it, and it's much easier to digest.

"All these problems around gluten that people are having are to do with the fact that most bread is leavened using industrial yeasts. This bread shouldn't really be eaten or produced. It's a commoditisation and a disrespect to food to make things like this. Food shouldn't be heavily mechanised. It's a disservice to all of us, but un-fortunately people prioritise business over the food system."

Initially working as a nomadic baker, proving loaves in a friend's basement and baking them in a local restaurant's wood-fired ovens, Mackinnon worked on perfecting his bread recipes, knocking on doors and selling them to local households in Hackney. His flavourful bakes became such a hit that he built up the confidence to open his own shop, roping in a gang of committed, like-minded bakers, and the Bakehouse was born.

"I don't tend to say no, and people wanted the bread," he says. "There were a lot of people around at the time with great transferable skills and who wanted to come on board, so we grew very organically, with a cross-pollination of ideas really informing what we do. There's something very tangible and appealing about the work we do: dealing with fridges breaking and pots of bread bubbling away, it's difficult not to want to join in. You never do the things you do if you know what's involved beforehand. We weren't bound by preconceptions."

Mackinnon hasn't looked back, but his renewable energy background still comes into play in his business, where the focus is on low environmental impact and sustainability. All of the energy in the Bakehouse comes from renewable sources; bread is entirely hand crafted, delivered to local businesses by a Dutch bicycle; and

everything from food to furniture is recycled.

The provenance of the different flours that go into the bread is a key and ongoing concern, with Mackinnon working with specialised millers of stoneground, organic flour in Dorset, Gloucestershire and Northumberland. The bakery is even milling its own grain in the arch next door with a stone mill, and – due to frustrations at the lack of organic, mill-quality grain available in the UK – growing its own wheat, oats and buckwheat in Suffolk.

"We're committed to using organic, British grains that support our ethos of being a deeply ecological bakery, but that is much harder than it should be, and the grain isn't easily available. I want to work directly with farmers and create that demand, and setting up our own small farm where we can experiment has allowed us to have a much more educated viewpoint when we have that dialogue with farmers.

"All the wheat research is aimed at big agribusiness, there doesn't seem to be the funding for organic, so that's what we're exploring in Suffolk. We've just sown a very interesting Danish organic wheat grain; an old, heritage variety which has good flavour and deep roots which draws out more nutrition and micro-nutrients with exciting things in them. It's brilliant to have a go at that."

Mackinnon is clearly consumed by his quest to improve the way we make and eat bread, and his day-long bread-making classes at the Bakehouse are booming. "I'm incredibly proud to be a baker, and I want us to have more bakers," he says. "Bread has been the backbone of our communities for years and I want to restore the skill and respect back into it."

E5 Bakehouse:
Arch 395
Mentmore Terrace
London E8 3PH

Website:
E5bakehouse.com

Follow:
@e5bakehouse

155

The Clove Club

"We have tried to create a restaurant for our generation."

Daniel Willis, Co-founder.

The Clove Club is a restaurant that has changed the British culinary landscape far beyond the confines of Shoreditch, where it sits twinkling and resplendent in the glorious former Town Hall building. Featured in the San Pellegrino 'World's 50 Best Restaurants' list every year since it opened in March 2013, and awarded a Michelin star a year after opening, it's an eatery that not only draws diners from across London, but also top chefs from around the world.

Glaswegian chef-owner Isaac McHale's cooking background includes stints at Noma in Copenhagen, Marque in Sydney and six years at the helm in the kitchen of The Ledbury in London, but it was cooking above notorious East End boozer The Ten Bells in Spitalfields with James Lowe (Lyle's, p.32), as part of self-styled cooking duo the Young Turks, that brought the plucky chef's own unique talents to the fore.

There was such an overwhelming appetite for Isaac's creative, modern British cooking, typified by his famous dish of buttermilk fried chicken with pine salt made with foraged pine from East London parks, and appreciation of the relaxed, mischievous front-of-house style of co-founders Johnny Smith and Daniel Willis, that the trio successfully part-crowdfunded this, their first stand-alone restaurant. It's one of the first of a fresh flush of restaurants to shake up dining in the area of Old Street, once a part of town you'd head to for its bars, clubs and cheap Vietnamese BYOs rather than to experience cutting-edge cuisine in a cool but brilliantly grown-up environment.

The Clove Club has grown out of long-established friendships (Daniel and Johnny go back to nursery school days in Stockport) and its roots in East London predate its Ten Bells residency, as the first incarnation of The Clove Club began as raucous, debauched dinner parties in their shared house on Dalston's Sandringham Road. "We used to throw these wild house parties and make our own seafood platters and pork pies," says Johnny. "It got more civilised as we got older, but when we first came to London we were doing music and looking for places to throw raves and parties, and it evolved into dinner parties and supper clubs. We called them Clove Club after the old boys' society from the local school."

Daniel explains how this has influenced the vibe of the restaurant. "Music is still a really big part of what we do. A lot of restaurants don't consider what's being played in the background, but we do. It was always a big part of The Clove Club in the flat and it's followed through to the restaurant. Our service style harks back to those days of welcoming people into our home too. That's what took people aback and that's what we try and recreate here in terms of service. The ethos has stayed the same, but what we've learned between then and now is how to run a business, which we had no idea of back then!"

The restaurant encapsulates a new mood for top-drawer gastronomy combined with a laid-back atmosphere. It's somewhere you can nip into and sit at the bar with a cocktail and snack, perhaps a plate of Isaac's house-cured hams that hang above the dining room's vast windows; or go all out for the extended nine-course dinner menu, exceptional value at £95. However you choose to experience this restaurant, you'll be delighted by the effort, skill and originality at work in every single element.

Isaac works tirelessly to find specialist suppliers that help drive the restaurant forward, people like his citrus grower in the South of France who grows over 250 different varieties like lemonade fruit, kabosu, blood mandarin, hana yuzu and Tunisian bergamot. He uses these obscure and flavourful fruits deftly to add new and interesting notes to his dishes.

Co-owners Daniel Willis, Isaac McHale and Johnny Smith.

"You can have really well-considered, ambitious food without having to pay through the nose, or feel like you shouldn't be there."

"There's care and attention to detail but not the silverware and associated costs," says Isaac, who works with number two Tim Spedding on menus that are as likely to reference heritage Scottish flavours like 'reestit mutton' (Orkney, Shetland-style smoked, dry-cured mutton legs, traditionally hung in the rafters above peat fires) as they are the Indian spices he grew up with in Glasgow. "I came from a long time at The Ledbury where we were doing things in a certain way, and now I'm looking at things differently. In order to be new we couldn't copy what had come before; it had to be ours. We all live east, this is our part of town, so it feels right."

"It feels like we're in a whole new phase of rediscovering British cuisine," says Daniel. "There's a whole generation of people like us who went to really stuffy, high-end fine dining restaurants and felt like we were slightly uncomfortable, and like we didn't belong there. And our frustration with that informs what we do. We said, 'let's create a restaurant for our generation', and that's what we've tried to do. You can have really well-considered, ambitious food without having to pay through the nose, or feel like you shouldn't be there."

The Clove Club:
Shoreditch Town Hall
380 Old Street
London EC1V 9LT

Website:
thecloveclub.com

Follow:
@thecloveclub

Buttermilk fried chicken in pine salt. See recipe section at back for details.

Towpath

"Our business plan was based on the intuition people would like it. There was no real plan."

Lori De Mori, Co-founder, pictured (left) with her daughter Michela.

166

It's rare, even radical, for a restaurant not to have a website these days, but there's an almost daring simplicity to the Towpath café on the Regent's Canal, which underpins its charm. From March to the end of November you can sit at its tables and savour something very special. Whether it's a solitary coffee with eggs and mojo verde on toast for breakfast, or a lunch of whole roasted plaice with buttered new potatoes shared with friends, every element of your meal has been carefully considered by founders Lori De Mori and Laura Jackson.

Created in 2010 by Lori and her then-husband, food photographer Jason Lowe, Towpath started as just one tiny unit, and has since expanded to four. "There was nothing else here when we opened," says Lori, who at the time was living in a flat across the canal with Lowe, having moved over from the Tuscan hills where she had written four books about Italian food and food culture.

"I was writing but I wasn't making a life for myself because my kids were grown, and I wasn't really meeting anybody. I thought, 'I'd like to do this, because what a good way to meet people.' I'd just done the Camino de Santiago, a huge, 900km pilgrimage across Spain, where you carry all your stuff on your back and I was very big on what actually makes people happy, and how little you actually need, so I was intrigued about playing with this space. I thought that people would like a place in London with a genuine welcome, that doesn't have internet or takeaway, where you just have to come, and here it is."

Jason Lowe had met chef Laura Jackson while she was cooking at a friend's auberge in France, and was just finishing up and looking for opportunities back in London. "I had this idea there would be nobody down here, I'd be writing while waiting for the occasional customer to have a piece of cake, which was not the case at all.

Meeting Laura was very serendipitous: she was keen and talented and about to leave the middle of nowhere to come back to London, so it just seemed like a really good idea."

"After three months we said, 'let's just see what happens.' The business plan was the intuition that people would like it, but there was no real plan. We were cooking at home initially – she had to be so flexible and versatile, and it was hilarious, and a lot of fun. There were six people behind this bar at one point. I mean, I don't know how we did it."

While part of the genesis of the place, Lowe is no longer involved in the day-to-day, and Lori and Laura run the café together, with help from visiting and part-time chefs such as Rachel O'Sullivan (previously of Spuntino and Lardo, p.264), as well as Lori's daughter Michela, who flits between the bar and kitchen. "We joke that it's a sort of rehab for chefs who don't want to be in intense kitchens any more. And that Laura is my new wife," says Lori. "We're really, really in it together. In every sense, right now this is our place. We're quite a complementary team. If we wanted to close the Towpath and run it into the ground in three months we would put her behind the bar and me in the kitchen. Laura is one of the most naturally talented chefs I know, she's truly inspired and passionate."

"I'm really interested in people, for me that's the interesting thing – engaging with people and getting them to realise that they don't actually want what they think they want. They think they want Wi-Fi and a takeaway but they really want to sit down and just look at the canal for a minute, and eat something really delicious. It's changed so much around here, and it's so nice to be a part of this area. There's a real community which is wonderful – lots of creative people working their own hours, and lots and lots of friendships have been made."

Roast chicken with farro salad and aïoli. See recipe section at back for details.

" People think they want Wi-Fi and a takeaway but they really want to sit down and just look at the canal for a minute, and eat something delicious."

Though originally from LA, Lori's food philosophy is deeply inspired by her time living in Italy, where simplicity, freshness and seasonality are key. All produce comes from Leila's Shop in Arnold Circus, Shoreditch, which is renowned for its exceptional sourcing. "We feel like Leila's is a sister place to ours. She has a lot of personal integrity about what she wants to do and what she doesn't, and she's brilliant at finding really special suppliers. Everybody who we buy from are people where we think, 'if we did what they did we would want to do it like they do it.'"

As such, bread comes from the E5 Bakehouse (p.146), but much of what the menu offers is homemade. "We do try to make everything ourselves," says Lori. "So we're gathering elderflowers and making elderflower cordial, which is there for a period of time; we're making yoghurt and making all our own jams. And we don't have croissants and things, we have a really simple Italian olive oil cake which is a thing that my kids grew up eating."

Laura describes her food as "homely, not fussy", and, while the breakfast offering remains largely unchanged, she changes the lunch menu daily. "I plan my menu around what produce is good, and I'm cooking food I would love to eat," she says. "We're well known for our toasted cheese sandwich, and one of my favourite things to cook is roast chicken. In summer I do it with farro, peas, broad peas, mint, spring onions and lemon parsley dressing with aïoli. You pour all the gravy over the farro and it soaks it up like a sponge. That's pretty much me on a plate."

Towpath:
Regent's Canal
London N1 5SB

Between the
Kingsland Road
and De Beauvoir
Road bridges.

St John
Bread & Wine

St John Bread & Wine:
94–96 Commercial Street
London E1 6LZ

Website:
stjohngroup.uk.com

Follow:
@StJBW

This outpost of Fergus Henderson and Trevor Gulliver's seminal St John restaurant upped the dining game in Spitalfields when it opened in 2003 and has raised many a top London chef through its ranks. Both a bustling restaurant and a bakery shop selling the group's superb baked goods, you can breakfast here with grilled kippers, lunch on ox liver, or share a supper of pheasant and trotter pie. It also offers some of the best value small producer and natural wines to drink in or takeaway.

Growing Communities

" Eating something that's just been picked totally changes your perception of what food is all about."

Sophie Verhagen, Head Grower.

At the very top of Springfield Park, just north of Stoke Newington, concealed behind shrubbery and a slatted wooden fence, pear and apple trees flank bushy rhubarb plants; neat raised beds boast glossy chard, peppery nasturtiums and an array of lettuces. A polytunnel housing climbing courgette plants and cucumbers masks a border filled with raspberries, Japanese wineberries and mint, while in the Victorian greenhouse a fig tree wafts its green tobacco scent and tomatoes grow towards the vaulted glass ceiling.

Birdsong drowns out the sounds of the city in this thriving food oasis, and you could – as you pick your way through the organic, edible beds – forget that you're in the depths of Hackney, until you look up and see the backdrop of a neighbouring housing estate. This describes the scene at Urban Food Award-winner Growing Communities' Springfield Park market garden, just one of 12 small urban growing sites across disused land, church gardens and estates that make up the Hackney-based social enterprise's 'Patchwork Farm'. Every Tuesday, the garden is open to anyone who might like to come and volunteer to maintain it: watering, weeding and cropping the salad produce which is bagged up for the zero-carbon 'Hackney Salad' bag. These bags in turn find their way into local shops and restaurants, as well as forming part of the broader Growing Communities Bag Scheme.

Growing Communities was set up almost 20 years ago to promote a sustainable, re-localised food system to the people of Hackney. Through its organic farmers' market, which supports small-scale organic and sustainable farms and urban growing sites in and outside of London, and its bag scheme, it provides city dwellers with affordable, fresh, organic and seasonal crops on a weekly basis. The farmers' market takes place every Saturday at St Paul's Church in Stoke Newington and is currently the only fully organic market in London, and the bag scheme services over 1,000 households with organic fruit, veg and salad. A larger, community-run farm in Dagenham subsidises the bag scheme with produce, provides a full-time job for a grower, and experience and training for local volunteers.

Patchwork sites within London such as Springfield Park also provide this valuable experience, giving volunteers a place to come week in and week out. As its head grower Sophie Verhagen explains, "People come for a huge variety of reasons. I've got a couple of people who were made redundant earlier than they had hoped and they just needed to get out of the house. Sometimes people are thinking of going into horticulture and so they come and have a taster. Sometimes people just like gardening and they don't have a garden because they live in London and they just want to get their hands dirty. We have young, college-type people and people in their sixties: I think some of them find it quite therapeutic, while some of them like the social element. Being outdoors, learning stuff about growing … some people are particularly interested in that."

Website:
growingcommunities.org

Sophie Verhagen, Head Grower.

I'm delivering for
Growing Communities'
organic vegetable
box scheme

www.growingcommunities.org

Violet

"Baking deserves just as much attention to detail as cooking does."

Claire Ptak, Founder, pictured.

"When you're a good cook you know what to tweak to make it taste right, and that's what I apply to baking," says Claire Ptak, whose tiny, white stucco Violet bakery on Hackney's Wilton Way has become one of London's best-loved food haunts. "For me it's really instinctual: I taste something and I want that satisfaction. I want every bite to be a great experience. It has to be worth it."

Inside, her flour-kissed bakers work deftly in the open kitchen, rolling out pastry to encase wobbly custards for seasonal quiches, or creaming together butter and sugar for her unrivalled sponges. Dappled natural light spills through the window on to the vintage glass cabinet where piles of cookies, brownies and beautiful seasonal fruit tempt from their stands.

Ptak named her bakery after the sweet-smelling wild violets that captivated her as a child growing up in California, where food was always at the centre of family life. She began cooking professionally after studying filmmaking and realising that her heart lay in the baking she was doing before and after class. Landing a job in the pastry section of chef Alice Waters' Chez Panisse in Berkeley – one of California's most iconic and influential restaurants – was the start of a journey that would eventually lead her here, to a quiet street just off London Fields.

"What I want to do is create a symphony of ingredients and have those ingredients shine through. That's truly the thing I took from Chez Panisse. Alice said she didn't have a philosophy, but that's what she wanted to do and that's what she wanted to teach," she says.

Ptak spent three years under the tutelage of the veteran chefs at Chez Panisse, immersing herself in cooking, tasting and learning, but eventually leaving to join her partner Damian in London. She began working as a food stylist for national newspapers and magazines, while also selling her baked goods at a stall on the newly revamped Broadway Market. "We moved to East London because we could afford it, but also because it was an interesting place to be," she says. "There was definitely a sense that people were becoming more interested in better food."

Working out of her rented home kitchen, sourcing seasonal fruits and small-production stone-ground, organic flours as opposed to industrially produced ones, Ptak became known for her flavour-focused bakes on the weekly market stall, and began looking for a separate kitchen space to keep up with demand. In 2005 she found the charming, jewel-box site on Wilton Way, and though the initial intention was never to open a bakery, the hoards of locals at the door twisted her arm.

Though she's now surrounded by other small businesses, when the bakery first opened it was considered to be in such a remote spot that Ptak would have to drive around herself to source ingredients. But its location in this part of Hackney feeds into Violet's identity, with Ptak, who grew up foraging in California, heading to the nearby marshes for rosehips that find their way into her hedgerow jelly; fig leaves to infuse custards and ice cream; and elderflower for her homemade sodas.

She's found wild pears and mulberries growing on housing estates near the bakery, and also grows her own lemon verbena for things like her quick strawberry jam. She uses Leila's Shop in Shoreditch to source much of her produce, and raves about Leila's penchant for finding rare, exceptional ingredients like Corsican grapefruit. She's also a regular at the bakery's neighbouring Turkish-run grocery store.

"Anything you ask for, they get," she says. "They've got a great organic section, their fruit and veg is super fresh and they're amazing. They welcomed us on this street and they've been so

"I want every bite to be a great experience. It has to be worth it."

supportive. We really work alongside them, and I can't thank them enough because they could have been really dismissive of us but they are incredibly welcoming and helpful."

In a market flooded by over-iced cupcakes, Ptak's wholesome, tasty food has struck a chord, and in 2014 her *Violet Bakery Cookbook* was published to great acclaim. Her uniquely honed palate and her considered chef's approach to baking means that she's leagues ahead of many in her field, but she's also a born educator. The daughter of writers and teachers, she has a way of communicating her passion that's both infectious and totally at odds with much of the vapid baking content we're bombarded with.

"This huge resurgence of baking in the media has been good for business, but it has also created this whole new industry of cakes that are really bad! There's so much icing everywhere, it's all about 'the look' and the taste is totally forgotten. It's giving cakes this really bad name! I've always tended to like less sugar in things because I want to taste the ingredients, not just the sugar. I use sugar like I use salt in cooking, to bring up the flavour of something. If you taste something, and it's lacking, or it doesn't have the punch that it needs, adding just a teaspoon of sugar can bring that flavour up."

"Baking deserves just as much attention to detail as cooking does. Not just in the scientific composition of a baked good, where you're obviously having to balance things to get it to rise and to work, but also that you have to think about balancing flavour and making it delicious."

Violet:
47 Wilton Way
London E8 3ED

Website:
violetcakes.com

Follow:
@violetcakes

Wild garlic and feta quiche. See recipe section at back for details.

Rawduck

"I was struck by the romance of restaurants, the generosity of them and the feeling they give you. It became a bit of an obsession."

Clare Lattin, Co-founder, pictured.

Rawduck—E8

Rawduck is a light-flooded, plant-filled space alive with chat, the sound of vinyl playing and the smells of very good cooking. A well-priced list of natural and low-intervention wines is chalked up on the blackboard and there's a large, ramshackle shelving unit filled with a rainbow of housemade pickle jars, wine bottles and hand-crafted ceramics.

Nourishing, seasonal and global plates of food, from charred Welsh lamb chops to buttermilk chicken or miso and brown rice porridge with kombu, poached egg and bonito flakes reflect the wanderlust of co-owners Clare Lattin, Rory McCoy and Tom Hill, and can be ordered for breakfast, brunch, lunch or dinner. You can pop in for a snack and a carafe of wine, a decent coffee or even a stomach-settling drinking vinegar. It's brimming with influences from eating cultures as diverse as Japan, North America and Italy, and like its visionary co-founder, Clare Lattin, Rawduck has had more than one life.

What started out as a tiny, but fiercely popular café-cum-wine bar on Amhurst Road in 2013, was transported to its larger, more contemporary site on Richmond Road after the neighbouring Victorian terraced housing became structurally unstable just months after opening. "It's the last thing you expect to happen," says Clare, whose first restaurant, Ducksoup in Soho, was a runaway success. "It was very upsetting, because you put so much into opening a restaurant and we just had to evacuate – no one could ever get back in. It was like the *Mary Celeste* – you could still see all the wine glasses and plates of food just sitting there. The rats were having a riot."

Lattin and her business partners resurrected their Hackney plans, driven by determination to create a local restaurant in their own neighbourhood. "I did initially think 'it's never going to happen', but then afterwards I was like, 'no, no, we built that'. Everyone was so sad – people kept saying 'oh no, I loved that place' – you don't often hear that, people don't tell you those things, they usually just complain. I thought, 'God they loved it! We've got to do it again'.

And do it they did, with this ricochet of fate resulting in a much bigger space than originally planned. "The space is great, it means we can cook what we want to cook. The kitchen before was so tiny. There's a landscape here to be a little bit more diverse, and people really soak up the experiences you're giving them. People feel like they own it here in Hackney – there's a real sense of community, and when you do something people really take it on. I feel like East London is a very big community; you can go from

"Everything about it is creative, you're constantly thinking, 'how can we do this better?'"

De Beauvoir to Hackney Wick and sense that, whereas other areas of London feel more closed."

Lattin juggles her time between the restaurants and her restaurant PR company 84, but was head of publicity for the publisher Quadrille until she was 38, working with restaurants on their cookbooks. "I was definitely always a gannet, then I started to travel a lot and I was struck by the romance of restaurants, and the generosity of them, and the feeling they gave you. It became a bit of an obsession. In Italy and France, you can eat out on your own all the time, but back home it felt like it always needed to be a bit of an occasion – you couldn't just rock up and say, 'I want a really lovely plate of this and a glass of wine', and that's when I started thinking about opening Ducksoup."

And she hasn't looked back. "It's exhilarating, I love it. Everything about it is creative, because even on the business side, you're constantly thinking, 'how can we do this better?' It's not just coming into work, it's setting up, cooking, serving, it's constantly examining and analysing how you can make the business better. You've got to serve the community – they want to eat a nourishing supper, and they want it to be accessible, and they want it to deliver a mealtime solution for them, because they're eating locally."

"Being on the floor you get to really understand your customer – you see that you're giving pleasure to people and it's instant gratification. They're coming through your door, they're sitting down and you're making their night. That's a lovely feeling. It's lovely to see people coming back time and time again."

Rawduck:
197 Richmond Road
London E8 3NJ

Website:
rawduckhackney.co.uk

Follow:
@Raw_Duck

Smoked haddock and monk's beard fritters with cucumber and mint yoghurt. See recipe section at back for details.

Billy Franks

Website:
billyfranks.co.uk

Follow:
@BillyFranksCoUk

Self-taught, award-winning jerky producer Will Yates specialises in inventively flavoured jerky that he makes in Hackney Wick. Yates uses high-welfare, native-breed beef and turkey from Philip Warren Butchers in Cornwall and London's Turner & George, and is stocked by the likes of Whole Foods Market, Selfridges and East End pubs The Adam and Eve and Newman Arms.

Fin & Flounder

"We don't hide behind anything. We want our customers to be just as educated as us."

Danny Murphy, Manager, pictured.

"It's all about British and local here," says Fin and Flounder's manager Danny Murphy, who's been a fishmonger for more than 17 years. "It's all got to be sustainable – even down to the carrier bags we use, which are biodegradable. A lot of the day boats we use are in Cornwall – we have a guy called Martin who fishes mackerel, plaice and line-caught cod for us on his boat, the *Violet May* in New Haven. It's just one man and his boat and we get it the day it's caught – you can't do better than that in London."

A firm favourite among chefs and food lovers alike, Fin and Flounder wet fishmonger on Broadway Market is an old-fashioned fish shop with a forward-looking approach. Specialising in seasonal, sustainable fish and seafood, the tiny shop is known for its glittering array of daily changing sea bounty and its brilliant wine selection.

Mounds of glistening cod cheeks; oysters from Maldon; langoustine from Scotland; Dover sole and Cornish red mullet tempt from plinths of crushed ice, while in the fridges there's specialist oak-smoked salmon from Lambton and Jackson, if Danny hasn't given it all away. "The smoked salmon is just so unique," he says. "Sean Jackson cold smokes it all and it's got an incredible flavour. I open up packets on a Saturday for people to try in the shop, and I must give away at least a kilo – it's great for keeping people entertained while we clean their fish."

"I love talking to customers to help them find inspiration," says Danny, who worked for years as a fishmonger with L.F. Mash and Sons and at a fishmonger in Brixton Market before talking the helm at Fin and Flounder. "I'll ask them whether they want something sweet and simple, or if they're looking to show off a bit.

We'll work with them according to their budget and give them recipe ideas. Sometimes it's a case of – 'grab a couple of lovely bits of salmon, some wholegrain mustard and a handful of samphire' – that's a meal for less than a tenner and it will taste brilliant."

"Some of the fish, like the wild sea bass we get from Wild Harbour in Cornwall, or the fish we get from Kernowsashimi, comes in tagged. The customer can use the tag to check where the boat has been out to fish." Danny takes immense satisfaction in passing on the knowledge he's built up over many years in the trade, also training apprentices as part of Jamie Oliver's Fifteen apprenticeship scheme in the shop.

It's the details at Fin and Flounder that set it apart, from the care it takes in choosing suppliers, to the fact it enlists the help of top sommelier and wine importer David Harvey to choose wines that complement the haul. "Everything in the shop is related to fish and seafood, whether it's the spices, herbs and deli items we've selected, or the wine on the shelves."

Fin & Flounder:
71 Broadway Market
London E8 4PH

Website:
finandflounder.co.uk

Follow:
@finandflounder

Tayyabs

Tayyabs:
83–89 Fieldgate Street
London E1 1JU

Website:
tayyabs.co.uk

Follow:
@1tayyabs

Book a table to avoid the massive queue at this Whitechapel institution, and make sure you order the lamb chops and mixed grill, served spicy and sizzling, along with the fresh tandoor naan and rotis. Open since 1972 and still run by the same family, this place offers some of the tastiest and best-value Punjabi food in London.

Hill & Szrok

"We want to know that our animals have been roaming around outside and feeling the weather, eating the grass."

Alex Szrok, Co-founder.

Alex Szrok and Tom Hill, Founders.

The idea is so brilliantly simple, and such common sense, it's a wonder there aren't butcher shop-cum-restaurants all over London, but Hill & Szrok on Broadway Market is a completely unique offering. By day, the premium butcher's shop sells high-welfare, outdoor-bred meat and traditional sundries, but come 6pm the marble meat slabs are frantically cleaned down and the space morphs into a compact, twinkling restaurant serving some of the best meat in the capital.

Manning the kitchen almost single-handedly each night is young chef Alex Szrok, a graduate of acclaimed gastropub The Eagle in Farringdon, who steadily grills and plates his way through the busy service as chattering carnivores share seasonal plates and bottles of interesting wine.

It was while working at The Eagle with Luca Mathiszig-Lee that the pair found inspiration for the venture from an old-fashioned butcher's shop nearby. Luca left the pub to open The Three Crowns in Shoreditch before joining forces with Alex and butcher Tom Hill to realise their plan. "It's a chef's dream come true to be here," says Alex. "I try and spend at least a day a week working in the butcher's shop to keep my hand in. Watching Tom [Hill] working is brilliant because he's so incredibly skilled. It's such a craft; he's like a doctor."

Tom runs the butcher side of the business from Tuesday to Saturday, maintaining a dialogue with Alex that feeds into what he puts on the menu. "It's really a complete circle between the butcher and the restaurant – we use everything and there is essentially no wastage," says Alex, who uses bones to make stocks or jellies, making his own pork scratchings with pork skin, rendering down the fat from the scratchings to use as lard in pastry.

This resourceful nose-to-tail approach means that Hill and Szrok can afford to keep the prices accessible for the locals, while maintaining a homemade quality in everything they do. Alex relishes being able to take the lesser-known cuts and offal that don't sell so well in the shop to use for the restaurant, and to fashion into retail products for visitors to take home.

"It's brilliant to experiment with things I've never tried before. There's caul fat in abundance for developing my own signature faggot recipes and old-fashioned things like that. Among all that humble stuff – and I've fallen in love with offal – it's amazing on the flipside to have 120-day-aged T-bone steaks that weigh 1.5 kilos to cook and offer to customers. You don't see them in restaurants very much. To be able to cook a whole fillet of a cow to share is so rare – the quality is crazy."

"Watching Tom working is brilliant because he's so incredibly skilled. It's such a craft; he's like a doctor."

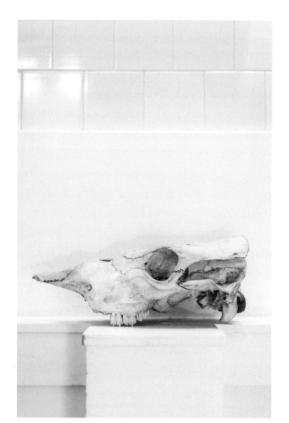

Having worked at The Eagle, where chefs take a hands-on approach to all aspects of the kitchen and restaurant, Alex was keen to keep a skeleton staff at Hill & Szrok, and works with just the two floor staff each night to cook for and service guests, sharing the kitchen porter duties between them. "It's pretty intense but quite slick now," he says. "Restaurants aren't busy all the time and I hate going to restaurants and seeing people doing nothing."

The menu changes on a daily basis, according to what's available, but because it's just Alex or his co-chef Jamie Allen in the kitchen each night they like to keep to a basic formula of intricate starters that can be made ahead, followed by a slow-cooked or braised dish and cuts of meat that just need a simple lick of heat from the grill. As such, you can always expect to find a terrine, pâté or rillettes followed by a catholic cross-section of meats and their different cuts, from pork chops to chicken supremes, lamb neck and rib-eye steaks.

The restaurant has also become well-known for its bigger, more opulent cuts like whole chateaubriands, half lamb shoulders and suckling pigs, as well as a generous selection of grouse, venison and pigeon during game season. Sides make the most of seasonal vegetables in dishes like British girolles fried in homemade butter, or roasted squash with goat's curd and roasted hazelnuts, while runny-yolked fried eggs are offered as an accompaniment to meats rather than technical, time-consuming sauces.

"The whole premise of the place is that it's simple," says Alex. "You can eat very cheaply or lavishly. A pork chop is £8.50, or you and a friend could share a £90 chateaubriand."

Provenance is absolutely key to the operation, and the three founders spent months in the run-up to the restaurant's opening in March 2014 visiting farms, meeting farmers and inspecting the animals. "Everything is proper free range and outdoor-bred. You can still have an organic animal that's been reared inside. We want to know our animals have been roaming around outside and feeling the weather, eating the grass. It's very important to us."

Hill & Szrok:
60 Broadway Market
London E8 4QJ

Website:
hillandszrok.co.uk

Follow:
@Hillandszrok

Warm lamb's heart salad. See recipe section at back for details.

Crate Brewery

"We're big on DIY – we like to do everything we possibly can ourselves. This is a reaction against chain bars and mass-produced food."

Neil Hinchley, Co-owner.

Founders Tom Seaton, Neil Hinchley and Jess Seaton.

Housed in the gleaming White Building on the edge of the Lea Canal, a few minutes walk from the Olympic Park in Hackney Wick, is Crate brewery, bar and pizzeria – a masterclass in the honest and underrated appeal of simplicity. Here, you can sit overlooking the water, supping on the brewery's own cask or keg beers – try the smooth, creamy golden ale or the toastier, maltier IPA – while tucking into thin-crust, stone-baked pizzas with inventive toppings like Middle Eastern lamb or sage and truffle.

Set on the ground floor of the Arts Council-funded centre for creativity, the bar and pizzeria's interior has been imaginatively and resourcefully decked out by local artists using reclaimed and up-cycled industrial materials from the local vicinity, including old railway sleepers, ladders and ratchet straps.

Opening a few weeks before the Olympics in 2012, Crate is considered to be one of the East End's first and most pioneering craft breweries, leading the way for a new generation of brewers and also championing other craft beer producers through its bar, whose beer list travels far beyond the few metres to its own on-site warehouse brewery.

Now producing an ever-evolving 20,000 litres of beer a week, with mainstays of its lager, pale ale and IPA, the genesis of this local spot was the result of a serendipitous chance meeting of minds, when former BBC radio broadcaster Neil Hinchley was introduced to siblings and café owners Jess and Tom Seaton through their cousin. "It was about a week in total between meeting each other and our offer on this building being accepted, but the planets just sort of aligned," says Hinchley, who had just quit his job, sold his house and been on a brewing course in the hope of starting his own brewery when he met his future business partners.

Locals Tom and Jess were already ensconced in the emerging food scene of Hackney Wick, running their café and coffee roastery Counter just down the canal, and together the three hatched a plan for the space. "We knew we wanted to do something a bit different, something very bespoke, because we're just overwhelmed by chain bars and restaurants these days, and this is the antithesis to that," says Neil.

"It was really important to create a place where we'd want to hang out ourselves, which wasn't a sterile environment," says Jess, who, along with Neil, has spent time as head brewer during the lifespan of the brewery, and who came up with the pizza recipes with her mother in their home kitchen.

"It was really important to create a place where we'd want to hang out ourselves."

"You never really stop developing. Even though we've been brewing for the last three years we still tweak every single recipe that we make every single time we brew it."

"Craft beer was a very new thing in London when we first opened," says Tom. "And luckily, we've grown with the market, but if we were to open a brewery now there is no way that we would try and brew it all ourselves! We learned the lessons early! You never really stop developing. Even though we've been brewing for the last three years we still tweak every single recipe that we make every single time we brew it. We're dealing with natural ingredients and methods so things change every time we do it."

Proving that they like to stay way ahead of the curve, more recently the trio have taken their skill for fermentation a step further by adding kombucha (a kind of fermented tea) to their repertoire with the launch of Jarr Kombucha, a separate brand, retail space and bar within the warehouse development. A great alcohol substitute, the funky new brew is available from the cocktail barge which is moored next to the brewery.

Crate Brewery:
7, The White Building
London E9 5EN

Website:
cratebrewery.com

Follow:
@CrateBrewery

Testi

Testi:
36 Stoke Newington
High Street
London N16 7PL

Website:
testirestaurant.co.uk

Follow:
@testiocakbasi

The stretch between Green Lanes and Stoke Newington is well-served by Turkish Ocakbasi restaurants, and everyone has their favourite. Stoke Newington's Testi, with its thrown-to-gether interior and smoking charcoal grill, is ours. Don't miss the chicken shish, or whole grilled quails. Mains come with an unbeatable charred-onion and pomegranate salad and warm Turkish bread, dredged in meaty grill juices.

Sandows London

"Cold brewing extracts the acidity so you get that extra sweetness without the sourness. It's the best of everything."

Hugh Duffie, Co-founder.

SANDOWS
LONDON

Hugh Duffie and Luke Suddards, Founders.

"It's nice to be somewhere that feels inherently creative."

London didn't really do cold brew before friends Hugh Duffie and Luke Suddards founded their start-up, Sandows, selling nattily-designed glass bottles of the chilled, cold-infusion coffee. The two friends met working at TAP Coffee on Wardour Street – one of the capital's most pioneering speciality coffee shops – and realised very quickly that their future lay in the cooler caffeine fix.

"We used to make cold brew there for the summer menu at TAP, and from one year to the next it got really popular," says Hugh. "We thought we'd just make some and sell it in the park, but then we realised there's quite a lot to it, so we decided to just bite the bullet and start up properly."

They spent months customising their brew using an overnight immersion method infusing fresh, light-roasted coffee in cold water for 16 hours. The reverse osmosis filtering of the water strips out the mineral content, just adding back in the desired amount and leaving more space for the flavours of the coffee.

Hugh used his background as the roaster at TAP to perfect the process. "The coffee has been roasted, but only just enough to bring it out of being green, and bring out the sweetness but then stopping rather than imparting roasted flavours," he says. "Roasting like this can make coffee taste sour or acidic, but cold brewing extracts the acidity so you get that extra sweetness without the sourness. It's the best of everything."

The result is a beverage with a wonderfully clean, fruity flavour that works both as a drink in its own right, and as an ingredient for coffee-based cocktails and drinks. Citing the Kernel Brewery and its weekly pale ale as inspiration, the pair source coffee which is as fresh as they can possibly get, working seasonally with coffee supplier Assembly Coffee.

"We like to keep it as fresh as possible, so keeping the amount of time between it being grown, processed and roasted to a minimum. It's then freshly ground a minute before we start brewing it for the best possible flavour, because coffee goes stale as little as twenty minutes after grinding."

"We've managed to take this speciality coffee to the mainstream, and that's really exciting."

The two young entrepreneurs initially based themselves in a space at Vagabond Coffee on Holloway Road, and began peddling their wares around local shops and restaurants. The response was so overwhelming that just a year later they managed to crowd-source £125,000 on Crowd-Cube to set up a production unit in Hackney Wick, employ staff and upscale their brewing tanks. "It's nice to be somewhere that feels inherently creative," says Hugh of their space. "We're round the corner from our designers Studio Thomas, from Crate Brewery, and Howling Hops. There's a real sense of community."

The pair have also expanded their offering to include Nitro cold brew – coffee which is charged with nitrogen and pours like Guinness. As well as being stocked in local cafés and shops, Sandows now holds pride of place in Selfridges and Fortnum and Mason, flying the flag for British coffee innovation. "We've managed to take this speciality coffee which is usually only found in trendy cafés to the mainstream, and that's really exciting."

Sandows London:
55 Wallis Road
London E9 5LH

Website:
sandowslondon.co.uk

Follow:
@SandowsLondon

Brawn

"I like the responsibility of having a neighbourhood restaurant. The menu has to be democratic in that way."

Ed Wilson, Founder.

Ed Wilson, Founder.

"It's about eating ingredients and drinking wines that are produced sustainably, with respect for nature and for the environment in which they are grown or raised."

On London's ever-revolving carousel of restaurant openings it can feel like something shiny and new appears every day, so it's a rare and special thing when one of them manages to captivate the capital's fickle appetites and make a lasting impression. To become a favourite place that people return to again and again is an even tougher call, but that's exactly what Brawn has done since its impactful opening in 2010. It is, quite simply, one of the best destinations in East London, if you are remotely interested in eating and drinking well.

Situated on the ground floor of a striking corner building on Columbia Road – a Shoreditch street famed for its weekly Sunday flower market and Victorian shopfronts – Brawn started life as the second in a small group of wine-led restaurants owned and operated by wine importer Les Caves de Pyrene. The group's former chef Ed Wilson, who made a name for himself opening its original outpost, Terroirs in Charing Cross, loved cooking at Brawn so much that, in 2015, he bought the restaurant from the group to run independently.

"I've come full circle with this place," he says from his favourite perch on the bench just outside the front dining room. "We opened this place after Terroirs, purely due to the fact that I lived around the corner and I knew the guy that ran it before. After seven years of cooking for the group I wanted to go back to taking one restaurant that I love dearly to being as good as it can possibly be.

"It's wonderful being back on Columbia Road, cooking for the community, as well as tourists and people who come from around the world to drink the wines we've sourced and eat the food we cook. This is my favourite bench in the whole world! It's so tranquil – apart from on a Sunday."

Though originally from Wakefield in Yorkshire, Ed spent a lot of time in the East End as a child. His dad had a flat in Hackney, and he's lived in the east of the city since moving down 18 years ago, and is very motivated by the idea of cooking for locals. "I like the responsibility of having a neighbourhood restaurant," he says. "The menu has to be democratic in that way." As such, Brawn is the sort of place you can pop into for a plate of well-made terrine and a glass of thoughtfully-sourced wine for under a tenner; or you can rely on it for a special occasion blowout meal (and one of the best Sunday lunches in London).

Seeking out exceptional ingredients to work with is at the heart of what Ed does, and over the years he's built relationships with obsessive specialist suppliers: people like his black pudding producer Christian Parra, whose award-winning *boudin noir* comes from Bayonne in the Basque Country of southwest France, and is studded with meltingly soft morsels of meat and unctuous fat. Brawn's intensely flavoured unpasteurised butter comes from Nantes, and has become a draw in itself, while its fresh mozzarella and ricotta is made in Campagna on a Thursday and flown in on a Saturday. "No one else in London is getting anything anywhere near it," he grins.

The wine is as important a part of the experience as the food, and the same approach to sourcing applies, making for a wine list that's a broad church of flavours and colours, many made by small producers working naturally and farming organically, with minimal intervention from the winery. Ed's time working with Les Caves de Pyrene has clearly informed his ethos, which he describes as "celebrating the ingredient, rather than transforming it", citing meals eaten on vineyards as his biggest inspiration.

"The food that's excited me the most has been when I've been sat at a wine-maker's table eating dishes that are rooted in the region, and drinking wine also from that place. That for me is where the magic happens. Ultimately that's what I want to do here. It's about eating ingredients and drinking wines that are produced sustainably, with respect for nature and for the environment in which they are grown or raised – whether it be animal, vegetable or grapes – and that reflect the region in which they are produced. It's about delivering something that makes people go 'wow', and then understanding the link to where it has come from."

Brawn:
49 Columbia Road
London E2 7RG

Website:
brawn.co

Follow:
@Brawn49

Duck hearts, sweetcorn and walnuts. See recipe section at back for details.

Lily Vanilli

Lily Vanilli:
6 The Courtyard
Ezra Street
London E2 7RH

Website:
lilyvanilli.com

Follow:
@lilyvanillicake

Simply put, Lily Jones is an artist, and cake is her canvas. The self-taught baker and cake designer also knows a thing or two about making her creations taste delectable, as witnessed by the droves of people who come to her bakery off Columbia Road for a slice. Her striking, seasonal cakes are decorated with everything from crab apples to glittered strawberries.

Pavilion Café

"It's about bringing fantastic producers to a park café and really exceeding people's expectations."

Rob Green, Co-founder.

It's true that the Pavilion Café, which sits on the edge of the boating lake in Victoria Park, has one of the most serene settings in East London, but the freshness, integrity and deliciousness of the food there is enough of a draw in its own right. Opened in 2007 as a joint venture between tea importer Rob Green and restaurateur Brett Redman, the idea was to create a community café that went far and beyond the usual offerings of a park greasy spoon.

Rob had returned from working as a social worker in Sri Lanka and was selling tea from an organic estate he worked with there at Borough Market when he met Brett and the two hatched a plan to bring some of the first-class produce from Borough to Hackney.

"When we opened, the East End was still a bit of a food void," says Rob, who now independently runs the café and its sister slow-fermentation bakery on Broadway Market. "We wanted to bring in all this really good produce like Monmouth coffee, good bread and cheese. It was about bringing fantastic producers to a park café and really exceeding people's expectations."

Finding the best ingredients to base the menu around was a starting point for building a business that takes an uncompromising approach to looking after the locals, providing them not just with a sensational backdrop for brunch, but a seriously memorable plate of food. Today the café relies on a strong network of suppliers including the Ginger Pig butcher, Northiam Dairy and Perry Court biodynamic farm in Kent, as well as Rob's Sri Lankan contacts and its Broadway Market bakery which provides all the delectable baked goods and the acclaimed sourdough.

The all-Sri Lankan kitchen team, which has been with Pavilion from the beginning, has earned the café a reputation for its brunch hoppers (fermented coconut milk and rice flour pancakes), sambals and breakfast curries. Aesthetically, the café owes much to the creative talents of in-house designer Rachel Gale, who sketches the ever-changing menu boards and curates the branding, pottery and furniture.

"It's more than just a job for me, and it's more than just a café. It's my life."

"It's the people's park, and I've always provided tea for a quid."

The beauty of the Pavilion Café is that it applies the concerns of a high-end restaurant to its sourcing ethos while delivering the accessibility of a café, something Rob was adamant about from the beginning. "It's the people's park, and I've always provided a tea for a quid and a piece of cake – everyone can come and have a cup of tea. I had a tea business and I'm an ex social worker, so I'm still very attached to the ritual of having a cup of tea!"

"I love the park life and diversity of customers – the dog walkers and young mums. It's so diverse and so interesting, and we're a real part of the community. My customers are my friends and we have a very core following." Rob fully intends to make the most of the remainder of his 10-year lease, and plans for a 100-seat covered deck extending into the lake are afoot. "We're perched on a lake; it's very rare to have such a beautiful physical thing right in front of you, and I want to go further and make it even more beautiful."

Pavilion Café:
Victoria Park
London E9 7DE

Pavilion Bakery:
18 Broadway Market
London E8 4QJ

Website:
pavilion-café.com

Follow:
@pavilionvicpark
@pavilionbakery

Café Spice Namaste

"When we first moved to Hackney people from our community didn't want to associate with us. They thought Hackney was dangerous."

Cyrus Todiwala, Owner, pictured (left) with his wife Pervin Todiwala.

Bombay-born, Parsee chef Cyrus Todiwala has been living in Hackney and cooking at his restaurant Café Spice Namaste in the City for over 20 years. In that time he's built up a reputation as one of the UK's most respected and cherished chefs, earning a host of coveted honours including an OBE and BBC Food Personality of the Year.

But it's his contribution to changing perceptions of Indian cuisine in the UK for which he is perhaps best known. Having been executive chef for the Taj group of hotels in his hometown of Mumbai before he came to the UK with his wife Pervin, Todiwala is an authority on different styles of Indian cuisine. "I learned a hell of a lot in Bombay," he says.

"The city's position as the financial capital of India means that it's a melting pot not just of different cultures, but of different styles of Indian food. You have all this incredible diversity in one place, so I was cooking everything from North Indian, South Indian, East, West Indian and Mughlai food from the Mughal influence. I was exposed to so much variety and different foods working for Taj and had to be incredibly reactive – I had to read and research a lot, and in those days it was pre-internet – you had to refer to books and go to libraries to find recipes."

It was shocking, then, for a chef with such an in-depth knowledge of Indian food to find, on arrival in the UK, that he didn't understand the so-called Indian food being cooked here in London. "I came over to run a restaurant for someone else originally," he says, "but what it ended up becoming was an experience of education. It was an education for me to learn that the Indian food served here was not Indian at all. It really confused me. I was scared at the time because I didn't recognise the food at all, so I started the whole process of cooking the food that I knew was Indian and it landed up becoming an exercise for educating diners and people around us."

Café Spice Namaste opened on Prescot Street in 1995 and has become a firm favourite among locals, families and City workers, thanks to Todiwala's deft hand with spicing and his delicious renditions of both classical and modern Indian dishes. On the menu you'll find classic Bombay street food dishes such as *bhael poori* (puffed rice mixed with tamarind, crispy chickpea vermicelli, pomegranate and finely chopped shallot) alongside spiced, tandoor-cooked wood pigeon or Parsee-style chicken curry with rice and potato or chilli cheese naan.

While he's a master of the nuances of Indian spicing, working with prime, seasonal British produce is key to Todiwala's cooking, and he's an enthusiastic champion of underused meats and heritage British breeds, being a patron of the British Lop Pig Society (Lop being one of the rarest pig breeds). He's also on a mission to cook and popularise goat, using the meat – a by-product of Britain's burgeoning goat's cheese industry – on the menu wherever he can. "It's terrible how much goat gets wasted," he says. "The males are used solely to impregnate the females so they can make milk, so thousands and thousands of them get killed and it's such a waste."

As such, spiced tandoor-cooked goat chops and fiery goat curries are a regular at Café Spice

"Look at Hackney now! It's a totally different ball game."

Namaste. "It's got a really delicious, distinctive flavour and is very in line with what we do in India because there we call goat 'mutton' and cook with it all the time."

While he and wife Pervin originally moved to Hackney out of necessity – it was where his first restaurant's staff digs were – the couple have chosen to stay in the borough, bring their children up here and open a community café in Victoria Park, near to where they live. Run by their son Jamsheed, who's following in his parents' footsteps, it specialises in Indian breakfasts and omelettes, samosas, Indian wraps and sandwiches.

"When we first moved to Hackney people from our community didn't want to associate with us. They thought Hackney was dangerous, and in the back of beyond. But we have a great community feel there, our neighbours are fabulous and we're not going anywhere. Look at Hackney now! It's a totally different ball game."

Café Spice Namaste:
16 Prescot Street
London E1 8AZ

Website:
cafespice.co.uk

Follow:
@CafeSpiceNamast

260

Sông Quê Café

Sông Quê Café:
134 Kingsland Road
London E2 8DY

Website:
songque.co.uk

This kinetic canteen is one of the best of Kingland Road's many Vietnamese restaurants: the queue snaking out of the door proves it. Owner Anh Phuoc Thi Pham's steaming bowls of *pho* come with seven different herbs, and her punchy chilli and garlic soft-shell crab is unmissable, as is grilled beef in betel leaf. Originally from Bến Tre, she trains each chef in the kitchen, teaching them her well-honed recipes.

Lardo

"There's something very simple and humble about curing meat: it has a quality and credibility to it which really appeals to me."

Eliza Flanagan, Founder.

Eliza Flanagan, Founder.

To sit at the bar opposite Lardo's hand-built, mirror-ball pizza oven as it belches out perfectly-charred, imaginatively-topped pizzas has become one of Hackney's simplest and most sating food pleasures. Named after the silken cured back fat of the pig, this neighbourhood spot, with its bespoke charcuterie and seasonal small plates, has been a trailblazer for outstanding but relaxed dining in the area.

"There was nothing here when we opened in 2012," says founder Eliza Flanagan of the stretch of Hackney's Richmond Road that houses the converted warehouse. The daughter of a wine maker and restaurateur father (who flew over from Australia to build the oven), Eliza grew up in restaurants in Adelaide, training in shoe design before what she describes as an "inevitable" return to hospitality when she moved to Hackney. Working closely with Pablo Flack and David Waddington, she was general manager of Bistrotheque (p.64) during the early noughties, when it was shaking up the East London scene with its theatrical, avant-garde brand of dining.

"I loved it at Bistrotheque. It was so exciting, but it was a special occasion place back then, and I felt the area also needed a really good neighbourhood place – somewhere people could go three times a week if they wanted to. There just wasn't anywhere like that at the time. I think the best things come out of a genuine need for something," she says.

Captivated by the idea of creating a restaurant "along the lines of an Italian pizzeria, but more", something informal yet somehow still exceptional, she left Bistrotheque and used money she and her partner had stockpiled to fund an epic road trip across America in search of inspiration. "We drove 8,000 miles in two months around the States, and I saw some really nice, professional, slick neighbourhood restaurants that were just doing things really well and being sustained by their local communities. That excited me."

The appetite for, and movement towards, home-curing and 'farm-to-fork' provenance that she also witnessed Stateside became a clear part of the vision for what would become Lardo. "There's something very simple and humble about curing meat: it has a quality and credibility to it which really appealed to me. I wanted to make the best charcuterie: to know the farmers, curers and the whole cycle."

While travelling, Eliza fell in love with charcuterie made from Mangalitsa pigs, a rare-breed beast prized for its extensive fat and marbled meat, making it perfect for curing. Working with local expert charcutier Matt Bedell, and Native Breeds, a curer based on the Gloucestershire/Welsh border, the team developed a range of charcuterie for Lardo using that, and other rare-breed pigs. The pigs sourced are raised by the farms for longer than is traditional in order to develop their fat, making for exceptional quality charcuterie that draws on Italian traditions while celebrating British husbandry.

The inventive selection at Lardo includes spicy 'nduja (a spreadable Calabrian-style sausage), fragrant fennel pollen salami, and supple coppa. This level of involvement with the products on the menu is a key part of the restaurant's ethos, and is what elevates it beyond an average local Italian: thought, care and sheer hard work go into crafting as many of the menu's offerings in-house as possible, including everything from its bread, doughs and pasta to simple cheeses and syrups for its signature chinotto soft drink.

While the charcuterie and signature pizzas are mainstays, Lardo's menu is ever-evolving, reflecting the seasons and the best available ingredients translated by executive chef Matthew

Cranston. In spring this could mean bowls of spaghetti with clams and wilted wild garlic; or pale green nettle tagliatelle in a creamy sauce; and in autumn antipasti of porcini bruschetta followed by wood pigeon, Russian kale and polenta.

In December 2014 the team opened Lardo bebè, the compact little sister to Lardo, on Sandringham Road, Hackney Downs, with a smaller, more focused menu of pizza and classic pasta dishes and takeaway available; while in 2015 Lonzo, "Lardo's cellar door" opened. "It's the third part of the triangle," says Eliza. "It's more about the production and educational side of our business – a space for us to make all of our baked goods, our pastas and sauces and offer little masterclasses."

"Sort of test kitchen, sort of production kitchen", from Wednesday to Sunday the bakery, salumeria, kitchen and wine shop offers a weekly set menu of small plates for under £10, such as squid with potato and bottarga, or hay-baked celeriac with lardy loin, along with a list of small-production Italian wines. As well as providing a dedicated space for catering and baking, each Wednesday there are free 'Lonzo Lites' sessions – post-work masterclasses that give an insight into everything from how to make ice cream and tortellini to regional wine tastings or the benefits of stone-ground versus roller-milled flour. "It's a little taster and insight into the practices and passion behind what we do."

Lardo:
197–201 Richmond Road
London E8 3NJ

Lardo bebè:
158 Sandringham Road
London E8 2HS

Lonzo:
5 Helmsley Place
London E8 3SB

Website:
lardo.co.uk
lardobebe.com
lonzo.co.uk

Follow:
@lardolondon
@lardobebe
@lonzoHQ

Wild mushrooms with cauliflower purée. See recipe section at back for details.

LIVE EEL
F.COOKE
HICKMAN
HOT AND JELLIED
EELS
NO SMOKING
STAFF
W ANTED
for
SATURDA

F. Cooke

F. Cooke:
9 Broadway Market
London E8 4PH

Though live eels fished from the Thames no longer writhe on its marble counter, the food and beautiful antique tiling at this Broadway Market stalwart remain virtually unchanged from its 1900 inception. Established by the Cooke family who still run it, this eatery is known for its handmade meat and suet pastry pies, mounds of fluffy mash doused in vivid green parsley liquor and chilli vinegar; and eels which come stewed or jellied.

The Marksman

"We come out of the kitchen and there are people we like. That makes it all worthwhile, because we work fucking hard."

Tom Harris, Co-head Chef, pictured (right) with Co-head Chef Jon Rotheram.

The saying 'too many cooks' does not apply at The Marksman, the historic Hackney boozer where best friends and co-head chefs Tom Harris and Jon Rotheram have been cooking their hearty, cravable British food together since April 2015. Walk in on the ground floor and you'll find a timeless pub interior with wooden tables and a long, lively bar serving pints to locals, but up one flight of stairs you're transported to an intricately designed modern dining room, vivid with hand-painted textiles, where tables can be reserved for lunch and dinner.

Down in the basement Tom and Jon are busy running one of the most exciting kitchens in East London, cooking everything from bar snacks and more refined small plates to full-blown roast dinners, drawing on the history of the setting – which has been a pub since 1865 – to create heritage-inflected dishes like the now-famous steamed beef and barley buns.

Chefs with calibre cooking in pubs is nothing new in London these days, but two head chefs tag-teaming in the kitchen? That's not something most pubs can boast. "A lot of people were worried, but we worked side by side at St John for eight years, so it's not like we don"t know each other very, very well," says Tom. "In terms of creativity it's such a boon to have someone to bounce ideas off, and to experiment on dishes with. We know each other so well that if I do a dish and it's not right he'll tell me it's shit, and vice versa."

Having discovered their cooking chemistry at St John, the pair began talking about opening a restaurant together, and after Tom heading up One Leicester Street and Jon working at Jamie Oliver's Fifteen, they reunited to find the right site. "We both live in East London and come drinking around here a lot, so it made sense to do it here," says Jon. "So many chefs have an idea and try and squeeze it into a space, but with this place the space has defined what we do. We wanted a pub, and a place with a great bar."

Aware that it was a well-frequented local with a loyal following, the chefs made an effort to retain the original look and feel of the pub downstairs, taking on its existing bar manager Kim Ottoway, and spending a lot of money making the space look very much like itself. "The building needed a lot of love," says Jon. "We rewired it completely, redid the ceilings and rebuilt the pub to make it sound, but we did very little to change the look of it."

"We didn't want to lose the locals," says Tom. "A business like this is based around its local community. Even though that community is changing we've managed to keep hold of the old boys who have been drinking here for 30 to 40 years, which is great. One thing that we really didn't want to do is turn it into a restaurant in what used to be a pub."

The layout means that the chefs can keep the downstairs for walk-ins, while upstairs the striking dining room, which was designed by local furniture maker Martino Gamper, is more like a conventional restaurant that takes reservations. The food itself is suited to both experiences, perfectly straddling the space between comfort and refinement with dishes like mutton curry (a play on Edwardian club curries), chicken and girolles pie and brown butter tart. Thanks to the culinary confidence of both chefs, these dishes have taken on a life of their own, becoming cult hits.

"We both love eating in bars so the food had to feel right in that setting, but it's still a little bit different from pub food," says Jon. "What's nice is that we have a couple of dishes here that have caught diners' imaginations and people have really fallen in love with them, which is what you want as a chef. You create a dish and you want it to be loved."

"Even though the local community is changing we've managed to keep hold of the old boys who have been drinking here for 30 to 40 years."

Over the past 15 years of cooking in London restaurants the pair have built strong relationships with some of the country's top suppliers, and, both being graduates of St John, they prefer to buy in whole birds, whole animals, or whole sides of animals to break down themselves. As Jon points out, "It's a lot easier to just find a butcher and say 'I want ten pork chops', rather than buying in a whole saddle and working out how to use it and what to do with the trim. There is a proper A-to-Z approach to it, it's about using your skills and teaching other people these important skills".

For Tom, being able to cook in an area he lives in and loves is a dream come true. "This is our community. Our friends drink here. One of the great things for me and Jon is that we come up from a busy night downstairs and there's always a few of our friends at the pub. That's why every chef becomes a chef. You start cooking for your family, you start cooking for your friends. We come out of the kitchen and there are people we like. That makes it all worthwhile, because we work fucking hard. That's important."

The Marksman:
254 Hackney Road
London E2 7SJ

Website:
marksmanpublichouse.com

Follow:
@marksman_pub

Chicken and girolles pie. See recipe section at back for details.